Stoicism-The Art of Happiness

How to Stop Fearing and Start living

Robert Miles

© **Copyright 2019 - All rights reserved.**

The content contained within this book may not be reproduced, duplicated or transmitted without direct written permission from the author or the publisher.

Under no circumstances will any blame or legal responsibility be held against the publisher, or author, for any damages, reparation, or monetary loss due to the information contained within this book. Either directly or indirectly.

Legal Notice:

This book is copyright protected. This book is only for personal use. You cannot amend, distribute, sell, use, quote or paraphrase any part, or the content within this book, without the consent of the author or publisher.

Disclaimer Notice:

Please note the information contained within this document is for educational and entertainment purposes only. All effort has been executed to present accurate, up to date, and reliable, complete information.

No warranties of any kind are declared or implied. Readers acknowledge that the author is not engaging in the rendering of legal, financial, medical or professional advice. The content within this book has been derived from various sources. Please consult a licensed professional before attempting any techniques outlined in this book.

By reading this document, the reader agrees that under no circumstances is the author responsible for any losses, direct or indirect, which are incurred as a result of the use of information contained within this document, including, but not limited to, — errors, omissions, or inaccuracies.

Table of Contents

Introduction..**10**

Chapter 1 ....**13**

What You Can Expect from Practicing These Stoic Exercises

- ❖ Main Benefits
- ❖ How to applies these exercise

Chapter 2 ....**21**

About My Experience with Stoicism (My Story)

- ❖ How I Have Failed
- ❖ The Challenges I've Overcome
- ❖ My Philosophy, Principles, and Values
- ❖ How I Have Overcome the Obstacles

Chapter 3 ....**28**

A Brief Overview on the Origins of Stoicism

- ❖ The Stoic Happiness Triangle
- ❖ Eudaimonia Live with Arete
- ❖ Focus on What You Control

Chapter 4 40
The Distinction Between the Two Types of Virtue

- ❖ Intellectual Virtue
- ❖ Expertise and Time
- ❖ Practical Virtue
- ❖ Result of Habit
- ❖ How to Recognize the Distinction
- ❖ When I Started Practicing this Distinction Living in Maintained Control

Chapter 5 53
Eliminating Absolute Self-Talk

Chapter 6 69
Do and Feel What is Appropriate in Every Circumstance

- ❖ Judging What is Suitable
- ❖ Accepting Circumstance Becomes Easier
- ❖ What it's Like Before you Recognized This
- ❖ How Things are Better Now as a Result of Practicing

Chapter 7 81
Only Your Judgement Makes Something Either Good or Bad

- ❖ Emotions are Based Upon a Judgement
- ❖ The Enchiridion
- ❖ Emotions That Are Restricting Your Advancement
- ❖ How This Strategy Changes Your Perspective

Chapter 8 94
Nature has Always Been and Will Always Be Outside of Your Control

- ❖ Our level of Influence on Nature
- ❖ High Influence Partial Influence No Influence
- ❖ How to Deal with Natural Processes
- ❖ Effectively Desires and Emotions are a Part of Nature
- ❖ How This Strategy Changes Your Perception

Chapter 9 ....**110**

Do Not Be Consumed by Your Passions

- ❖ Passion Can be the Enemy of Control if it's Not Contained
- ❖ How This Strategy Changes Your Perception
- ❖ What it's Like Before you Recognized This
- ❖ How Things are Better Now as a Result of Practicing

Chapter 10 ....**120**

Always Avoid Being Excessive or Deficient

- ❖ Accepting Nature
- ❖ Nonresistance
- ❖ Non-Judgment
- ❖ Non-Attachment
- ❖ How This Strategy Changes Your Perception

Chapter 11 ....**128**

You Deserve and Require Evidence, Reason, or Proof

Chapter 12 ....**136**

Putting it All Together1
- ❖ The Distinction Between the Two Types of Virtue
- ❖ Eliminating Absolute Self-Talk
- ❖ Do and Feel What is Appropriate in Every Circumstance
- ❖ Only Your Judgment Makes Something Either Good or Bad
- ❖ What will Start to Happen as a result of Practicing this Strategy What it's Like Before you Recognized This
- ❖ How Things are Better Now as a Result of Practicing

Conclusion..**144**

References..**148**

Introduction

Like all philosophy, stoicism has been taken and expanded upon since it first emerged in B.C. years. While you might have an understanding of what it is before going into this book, it's important to recognize that your perceptions should never be resistant to what is unknown. That being said, much philosophic work is up for interpretation. I encourage all readers to take these readings in their own words and apply them to their individual life while still being mindful of the complexities an oppositional perspective can present.

A stoic has long been thought as someone that is lacking emotion. Maybe it's the cowboy that doesn't seem phased when in a shootout. Perhaps it's the king that doesn't cry when his country is torn by war. Perhaps it's the martyr that doesn't flinch in the face of persecution. We have thought that stoics didn't have any emotion, but as we take you through the book, we are going to break apart that misconception. There are other myths we will discuss surrounding stoicism as well.

Stoicism is not nihilism. While it isn't a religion nor does it reject the idea of "nothing matters," that nihilists hold, it is still different from traditional nihilistic beliefs. Stoicism is what many see as the existentialism of nihilism without the cynicism. Some might think that stoicism can actually be somewhat of a response to nihilism.

You almost have to accept some level of nihilism to be virtuous. When you start to question, what is the point, what is my purpose, all of these existential questions, stoicism can help you define your philosophy, your virtue.

Stoicism is something that is going to be different amongst various groups. It's not about who knows the old texts the best, or how long someone has been a stoic. There shouldn't be arguing or attempting at proving oneself right.

There should only be discussing of various perspectives, because that is how true knowledge is going to be gained.

Stoics understand that discussion is important. They took their school outside to get people on the street involved in the conversations that might have seemed controversial at the time. I encourage you to take notes while you read of things you like, while also being mindful of the beliefs that might be more challenging. Talk with your friends about the reading and encourage others to look into stoicism so that you can have philosophical conversations much like those that laid the groundwork for these readings did.

Are You Feeling Stressed, Overwhelmed And Full Of Anxiety? You're Not Alone. But You Can Stop It...And Learn To Live A Stress Free Life.

Stress Is The Number One Cause Of Medical Problems Today. Anxiety Just Adds To Those Problems. But You Don't Have To Suffer Anymore! We Have The Answers You're Looking For!

Chapter 1

You Can Expect from Practicing These

Stoic Exercises

Before getting started, it's important that you are aware of where you currently are in your process with nature. Do you readily accept things as they come, or are you more resistant to change? One that is not in accordance with nature, those who are newer to stoicism, will often find difficulty accepting the natural flow of events. This includes things that are more challenging to confront, such as aging or death. There are other individuals who take things as they come, always ready for something new.

It's important to remember the difference between this and your level of bravery as well. Just because you are courageous doesn't mean that you are always accepting of reality. Being able to decipher between these elements is also important for your process with nature. Can you view things objectively? Those that have low self- esteem and often think negatively don't always see the reality of a situation. Similarly, some will dissociate from reality and avoid the challenging difficulties they face.

These people are the types that are out of accordance with nature. When there is resistance against the flow that things should be, how events unroll through time, then it only hurts the person that is resisting against the current. Wherever you are in your process with nature is perfectly fine, however.

You don't have to have all of the answers for how you're going to identify how in line you are with your process with nature either. Some individuals will find that they can better self-reflect after the event rather than be mindful while in it. A stoic will know how to find this balance, but wherever you are on the spectrum is perfectly fine.

What You Have the Ability to Do After You Read this Book

After you read through these texts, you will be able to better decipher between the things that are in and out of your control. You will have the ability to be mindful in a scenario while also knowing what it means to look deep in yourself and reflect on the situation after it has already happened.

One of the best ways to learn is through guidance rather than telling. It's a way to show reality in the eyes of the person that is doing their best to learn this new information. Throughout the book, we are going to guide you through the steps necessary to find the good life, the thing that all stoics are after.

We can't tell you an exact formula to get there. There is no supplement, quick fix, or easy solution. You will have to dig into your character and start to confront some things that might have been more easily suppressed in the past.

After this book, you will feel free from yourself. You will start to realize how uncomfortable it is to be in a place of constant resistance.

Whether it's trying to constantly battle yourself, or always looking for answers to the biggest mysteries of the world, you might have gotten comfortable in a place of misery. You can be certain there are always going to be upsetting things in the world, or material that is challenging to confront. In our society, it's easy to feed this perspective and validate our ideas that the world is a bad place. When we create so much negativity, it can make everything else challenging. We are always questioning "why" rather than looking at the "what" of what we actually have in front of us.

Why You Should Read it Now

We have fallen too comfortable in a place of unhappiness. But stoicism helps to change that. After some philosophers started to find that there was little point to many of life's pressures and grew into a place of nihilism, some scholars started to grow apart from this way of thinking. The cynicism was becoming too bleak, and in search of something better than just "nothing," many stoics started to create meaning through the idea of virtue.

After you read this book, you will find that it is easier to find happiness in all situations. The time to read this is now, because a virtuous stoic knows that all opportunity for knowledge should be taken. When we are given the chance to learn something new, we should take it for what it is. We can always find something new and useful in all experiences.

A stoic will understand that the only time that is wasted is when a lesson isn't learned. Even in the most horrifying, boring, or random situations, we can take something away. Whether it's an important memory, a mistake we won't make again, or exciting information that inspires us, there is value in all circumstance.

What You are Thinking

You might be thinking at this point that this sounds challenging, unachievable, or like total fabrication of something out of reach. To the wrong person, it could be. A stoic mind has to be one that is open at the very least. When you can start to consider that there is a black, white, and gray area in everything, then that alone can help to free your spirit.

Not everyone is going to be ready for the journey of a stoic, because it can mean going against some long-held beliefs that are hard to combat. What we think we know and what we know to be true is what has been taught to us through educational systems, what has been learned from observing others, and the messages we've collected from society. There are endless factors in which our views can be shaped by, because each small experience we have can be a moment which alters your perspective.

This is why some can be open to new thought processes, hopeful for answers to their questions, and others can be cynical, in denial of the future. There are numerous individuals that might find themselves in a place between both of these mentalities, and stoicism is a general philosophy that can provide answers to all individuals on the spectrum. It is not a religion, but for some, it might be. It is not a program that needs to be purchased, or a strict regimen that needs to be followed.

It is a way of thinking that helps to free up some of our anxieties. It is a lifestyle that embraces all things that come as they are, not in resistance to what is to be expected. It is one that encourages growth, knowledge, bravery, justice, and logic. Above all, it is a mindset shaped around virtue, which is inherently an idea behind many other religions, philosophies, and lifestyles.

Your Fears, Struggles, Challenges, and Day to Day Frustrations

Right now, like many, you might be struggling with day to day frustrations.

These include things like the guy that cut you off in traffic, a friend that's been getting on your nerves, bills that are going unpaid, kids, animals, and people online that are all too loud, and you never seem to get enough sleep. Your biggest fear of all, is that this is all there is to life.

What we don't realize is that we are frustrated at the car that cut us off because we're running late to work or having a bad day. That friend that is annoying us is someone we've been fighting with a lot, and we're scared one fight will be the one where we lose them. The bills that go unpaid make us scared that we're not going to have enough money to pay for the things we need to survive, and all the noise makes everything else that's bad even worse. We are frustrated and struggling because we are afraid, but our biggest fear is that we aren't going to be able to find the happiness needed to escape this situation.

Many people find happiness through money, and material things. Others enjoy the admiration of those around them and seek out fame whenever possible. It's a common mentality to think that the only way to find happiness is to have money. Money can help a lot of situations, but it will only ever bring stress relief, never happiness.

Main Benefits

All of these challenges that we are facing won't go away. That's not the point of stoicism.

It's not a get rich, pyramid, or any other sort of scheme to help you out of the struggles that you are dealing with. Instead, it's a mentality, a mindset, that is going to help you find the happiness that you've been longing for in the situation that you currently find yourself.

It's not something that's easy, but the benefits you receive will be clear. You might be faced with the challenge of not understanding the world, being unhappy with who you are, scared of the future, and regretful of the past.

What is to Be Gained After Reading

Stoicism isn't going to take away your actual problems but help you to find the mindset needed to actually face them head on and deal with them. When we are so caught up with how unhappy we are, it can feel like it's impossible to get out of the situation. Once you are able to find a place where you are dealing with the challenges, it becomes easier to find the solutions to break free from them.

When you can look at the root of an issue, it is what is needed to help it go away for good. There are some methods that can help alleviate anxiety, and get you feeling less stressed. However, you need to completely change your way of thinking if you want to see real results and long-term resolutions to the biggest challenges that you've been facing.

After reading this, you will discover that the things that used to make you upset no longer bother you that much. Rather than getting sick with rage or anxiety, you will feel that it's easier to work through your issues and get to the real reason that you might be feeling a certain way.

You will be able to practically apply these exercises to your life by getting into the mentality needed to alter the way that you used to think. You will start to find that it's easier to place emphasis on the things that matter most, while not letting the things that are out of control dictate how you will feel in this life.

How This Practically Applies to Your Life

Throughout the book, we are going to be providing you with mental exercises in the forms of stoic philosophy to help get you to a place where you are comfortable with even life's biggest discomforts. You will no longer have the problem of letting everything bother you. You won't have to worry about letting the little things get under your skin or being afraid over life's minor inconveniences.

Most importantly, you will feel free, true to yourself, and virtuous. The only thing that we have control over is our judgement, and that is how we will find that we can live in accordance with nature, on a path to virtue.

Chapter 2

About My Experience with Stoicism (My Story)

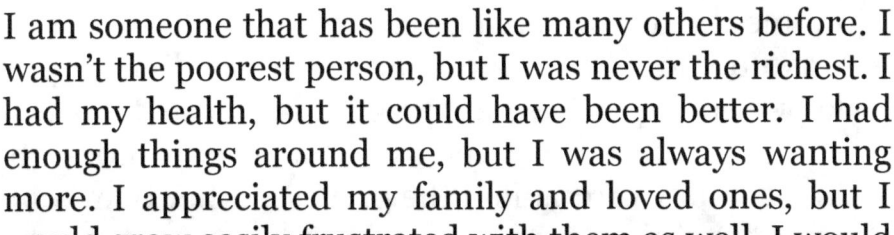

I am someone that has been like many others before. I wasn't the poorest person, but I was never the richest. I had my health, but it could have been better. I had enough things around me, but I was always wanting more. I appreciated my family and loved ones, but I would grow easily frustrated with them as well. I would let emotion get the best of me, and I would be driven by my passions.

I eventually got to a point where I couldn't take it anymore. I needed something better. I started reading about stoicism online, as strange as it might seem. Philosophy isn't something you would imagine popping up on chat rooms. Nevertheless, I got encouragement from others who were like me to continue to look into these subjects that seemed so interesting. Eventually, I started to really believe in what I was reading. I was going to the library and getting books from scholars that I never would have imagined I'd be reading.

However, there was still an issue. I was focused on something new, but I wasn't fully experiencing happiness. I was waiting around until I discovered some specific text and was hoping that I would eventually find the exact thing needed to tell me how I could be a happy person.

Then, I had my "stoic awakening," as I like to call it. This is different for everyone, and other stoics might not even experience them. That doesn't mean that they are any less philosophical. The way to describe it best is the moment that I understood stoicism. I realized that there was no endpoint or moment that I was living up to. I kept waiting to be happy, but the more I dove into stoicism, the more I realized that it was more about being happy throughout the process rather than waiting until the end.

It's kind of like how you might get more excited preparing for your first day of school, buying new clothes and supplies in anticipation, than the amount of fun you actually have on the first day of school. Stoicism is all about finding the happiness in the entire process, not just at one point after other work has been put in.

How I Have Failed

I failed in the past by wasting time hoping things would get better. I also failed by looking at my past mistakes and not being forgiving of myself. I would look at the choices that I had made and wished that I had done something different. I would lie awake in agony at night thinking about the past, wishing I could go back in time and make different choices.

I would sleep late on the weekends and go to bed early every night. I was sleeping my life away, and I didn't care, because my dreams were better than the bleak reality that I found myself in.

I was looking at everything in my life and seeing all the terrible parts, failing to see everything else that I had around me. I was never a particularly religious person, so I often found myself to be rather cynical, partially nihilistic. I would often think there was no point to anything.

My biggest failures were that I wasn't taking in all that I could from all the situations presented to me. Even when I did fail, or make a big mistake, those were all opportunities for me to learn and grow.

The Challenges I've Overcome

I have overcome the challenge of wanting to take the easy way out in my life. I used to indulge as much as I could. I would eat takeout, binge watch TV, and leave older projects behind because I was too busy distracting myself from the present. I liked to spend my money the moment I had it on things that would temporarily please me.

Through stoicism, I have been able to overcome this challenge. No longer do I give into my biggest urges and temptations.

Instead, I am focused in finding virtue, and becoming the person that I was meant to be all along.

I have overcome the challenge of always waiting for something to happen. I would fantasize about a better future, but part of me was always waiting for something to surprise me. I didn't realize that everything would stay the same unless I chose to make a better future for myself.

Why I am Passionate About What I Do

I am passionate about what I do because I know that it's the only way to be. There is no point in doing something as easily as possible. When we are focused on putting positive passion into everything that we do, that alone will make us virtuous. It gives us a purpose and something to be happy about.

When you can find passion in everything that you do, you will find virtue as well. When you can be a virtuous person, you will achieve happiness, or at least a state of contentedness even in the worst of times.

It's not as if you're going to be able to smile through someone's death, but you will be able to find meaning to keep moving forward after terrible tragedy has occurred.

Stoicism prepares you with the mentality needed to process even the most challenging of situations.

This is why stoics can be passionate about everything they do. Even when given a challenging task that they dislike, or that makes them question the point of existence, finding passion around that task helps to find purpose. If you can pull the reward from even the worst situations, it is much easier to navigate through this challenging life with ease.

What Separates Me

As someone that studies stoicism, I am unique because I understand the complexities that have created me. I am understanding of my presence in this world, and I am aware of how I relate to the spaces that surround me. As you begin to discover the principles of stoicism and how it can change your way of thinking, this becomes easier for all to realize as well.

My Philosophy, Principles, and Values

My philosophy is to always do what is best in the current moment. I have learned the difference between the things that I can change, and those that I don't have any control over. I am understanding of what is within my reach, and I know how to handle the negative feelings that come along with not having control over even the most challenging situations.

My principles include making sure that I have evidence behind all of the information that I take in, and that I am always questioning my own believes and virtues. The moment that I take things in at face value and don't look deeper into what they are, that is when I start to lose my virtue.

At the same time, I have to ensure that I am not weighing too much of my passion on the deeper meaning of what I discover as well, for that can sometimes alter my virtue as well.

My values include those that are grounded in growth, love, and happiness. The things that bring me joy and help celebrate love are what are most important to me. This includes family members, close friends, and the moments and memories we have together. I value anything that is going to teach me something, whether it's new knowledge about myself or the great world that surrounds us.

How I Have Overcome the Obstacles

The first step I needed to take to get here was to see the obstacles that were right in front of me. It's not that I am now immune to obstacles and can walk through them transparently.

Perhaps a true virtue could do this, but not me.

Instead, I am very aware of the obstacles that are there, and I know how to get around them. I also know that when I bump into an obstacle that I might have missed, that I have the tools required to pick me right up and keep going.

I am not a true, stoic, living with perfect virtue, and I have realized this. I still have moments where I make misjudgments, and sometimes I forget to question my challenging thoughts and act on emotion. I have also accepted that I might never be truly virtuous, but each step I take forward gets me further from my starting point. My true virtue doesn't lie within a point in time where I will reach a peak level of high morality; true virtue will emerge in the way in which one seeks virtue. It is not about reaching an end point. It's about aligning with time as it is passing, accepting of the bad, aware of the good, and focused on continual upward expansion.

Chapter 3

A Brief Overview on the Origins of Stoicism

Stoicism was founded by Zeno of Citium, who was of Phoenician descent. Unfortunately, there are only fragmentary quotations by Zeno available today.

Stoicism first appeared in Athens in the Hellenistic period around 301 BCE. Zeno taught in the Stoa Poikile (the painted porch). This is where stoicism got its name. Very little is known about Zeno's writings, and what we have gathered has been pieced together by his students and followers.

Zeno was followed by Cleanthes, then by Chrysippus, and still later by Panaetius and Posidonius. Only three ancient Stoics, Seneca, Epictetus, and Marcus Aurelius, survive in complete books. None of the first three philosophers ever had a large audience. Very little is available by any of these philosophers except in second-hand accounts (Sharpe, 2013).

Stoicism experienced an evolution from "living in agreement" to "living in agreement with nature," to "living in accordance with experience of what happens by nature." Stoicism is so versatile because it applies consistently to what matters at the present time. Though these philosophers all had their differences and helped to lay the foundation of stoicism, what we know to be true today will still differ from what they believed then.

We will get more into the three main philosophers, as well as other notable figures, in the last part of the chapter. First, before getting too into stoicism, we have to understand what the point of it all was.

The Stoic Happiness Triangle

Stoicism is all about being ok with what happens "by nature," even in confusing and/or uncertain times. Many people think the goal to being happy is to rid your life of anything bad. This is why so many people will go their entire lives unhappy.

The goal of the stoics is to live in accordance with nature, and from there, they will become virtuous. It isn't that they are going to be happy once they are virtuous, but rather, they find happiness in the process. Rather than waiting in misery to become happy, stoics know how to turn that misery into something productive, and from that change, positivity emerges, and perspectives change for the better.

Eudaimonia

At the core of the triangle is eudaimonia— the ultimate goal of life all ancient philosophies agreed on. Eudaimonia is a word that has been translated to have differing meanings, but at the core of it all, there are some things that this phrase has in common amongst interpretations.

Eudaimonia is what we are able to pull out from the bad times to be happy. It is a state that we are satisfied, content, and comfortable. We understand how to be joyous, and the small stuff isn't as bothersome. Eudaimonia has so many interpretations and is discussed so often because it will always look different in each individual, no matter what they believe in (Baltzly, 2008).

Live with Arete

Express your highest self in every moment. In order to be happy, we must constantly be putting our best selves out there. We should be using excellence in everything that we do, and we should never settle for anything less. To live with arete means that we know what it

is to have virtue, and we don't let ourselves to live without it anymore. Many stoics believe that this means that a person is living at their absolute fullest potential.

This is something that can be challenging to do, but it is a challenge that stoics embrace and will go after on their journey to the good life.

Focus on What You Control

Focus on the things we control and take the rest as it happens.

A stoic is constantly looking at the difference between the things that are in and out of their control. The reason that so many people will struggle to find actual happiness in their life is because they are trying too hard to take control where it doesn't belong to them.

This is also something that is going to be challenging, but still another thing that stoics will try to do often. As we take you throughout the rest of this book, remember these important three ideas. They are what makes up the triangle for what stoics are after in the first place.

Zeno

Died : c. 262 BC; Athens, Greece (several decades after stoicism founding)

Born : c. 334 BC; Citium (Cyprus Era : Ancient philosophy)

Zeno founded stoicism somewhat as a commentary on philosophical schooling at the time. Rather than forcing classmates to sit behind a desk for hours at a time, he instead chose to take his teaching to a public space, where he could say controversial things out loud to get people talking.

Zeno believed that happiness is "a good flow of life" or "living in agreement." He was a wealthy man that lost much in a shipwreck. From there, he decided to walk into a bookstore and took an interest

in philosophy. Stoicism emerged in Zeno because he wasn't able to buy into much of the cynical philosophies that he had already been reading. (Encyclopedia of Britannica, 2019)

Main Interests

Logic was important for Zeno. He often put an emphasis on making sure that his wise followers wouldn't fall victim to deception. Zeno was aware of the perceptions that we create and felt it was important for him to make others aware that they could alter this way of thinking.

Physics meant a lot to Zeno because he viewed the universe as God itself. Everything lived harmoniously together, and all the inner workings created one thing that we were all dependent upon. He felt that there was a divine fire, much like an energy that drives all the activity that exists in the universe.

Ethics were his final trinity of knowledge, and he felt as though there was only one good. Anything that caused happiness was to be achieved through reason, one universal logos that rules all. Anything that we feel that is bad would be pathos, and this is a disturbance in the natural flow of things.

Cleanthes

Died : c. 230 BC; Athens, Greece

Born : c. 330 BC; Assos School : Stoicism

Cleanthes became the leader of the stoic school after the suicide of Zeno. He was originally a boxer that found an interest in philosophy, listening to Zeno's teacher Crates the Cynic, and then eventually Zeno himself. He was a very patient person, and for this reason, some individuals even gave him a slow reputation. Some eventually gave him the nickname of "the ass," to which he actually responded well. He looked at this meaning that his back was strong, in fact, durable enough to handle whatever it was that Zeno would ask of him (Ellery, 1976).

Main Interests

Cleanthes knew that in the end, what was most important was "living in agreement with nature." He would discuss that even our bodies, in the sense that they are seperated from our mind, could be material possessions themselves. If we were in mental agony, then that could show on our body, which is how the two are connected.

He was a little oppositional to Zeno, as he believed that the divine fire which helped to keep all life going wasn't the earth itself, but the sun that provides us with so much power. Cleanthes also felt that any pleasure we experienced wasn't something that was good. In fact, he thought that it was going against nature and even "worthless."

This isn't true for all stoics, and we're going to dive deeper into this meaning throughout the book.

Chrysippus

Born: 279 BC, Soli, Cilicia (over a century after stoicism foundation)

Died: 206 BC, Athens, Greece

Chrysippus was actually another student of Cleanthes. He became part of the school after Zeno had passed, but he was still instilled with many of the same virtues. Chrysippus is said to have written 705 books. Through his writings, he was able to expand on what Zeno was taught, and he eventually became known as being the second founder of stoicism.

One interesting fact about Chrysippus is that he died from laughter. This alone is proof that the stoics don't have to be emotionless. Chrysippus amplified this to (among other formulations) "living in accordance with experience of what happens by nature." (Kirby, 2019)

Main Interests

Chrysippus was mostly interested in protecting stoicism. Not only did he help expand on the ideas, but he wrote them and shared them in a way that they were protected not only against the past, but of the future of stoicism as well.

He was known for his passion for education, and many thought it was even strange the amount in which he enjoyed learning. He ended up becoming head of the school as well after Cleanthes died.

Other Notable Stoic Influencers

The three scholars we just discussed were certainly important for the foundation of stoicism. However, we cannot overlook the others that eventually followed that helped to shape it as well. Throughout the rest of the book, we aren't going to get into the history as much and instead focus on the philosophy that was actually shared by these great scholars.

There will be quotes from some of the original stoics as well, but the intention of the book isn't to break apart history and instead take what is applicable to life now so that we can find some of the greatness that these individuals did.

If we stick too closely to their exact words, we will not be able to find our own path of happiness. We should be putting an emphasis on what the meaning behind what they said was, rather than logistically breaking it all apart.

Panaetius of Rhodes

He was the seventh leader of the stoic school that came along after Zeno had already died.

He helped to create a branch of stoicism that was a bit more eclectic.

Panaetius made changes in Stoic doctrines resulting in greater emphasis on personal duty, de-emphasizing the necessity for philosophical commitment in order to understand and achieve the Good Life. Rather than sticking to the strict ideas that other stoics had, he instead sought out to make it more applicable to an individual's life, so that they could take stoicism and use it practically.

Posidonius of Apamea

He was a stoic philosopher, astronomer, and geographer. Despite his skills, he still felt as though philosophy was the most important art of all. Even his most scientific of works were still things that were based in philosophy. He strongly believed that our passions were connected to our human nature. It wasn't our fault for these passions, but rather, the ethics that we believed, that were the issue for how we reacted to these intrinsic passions.

Lucius Annaeus Seneca

He was also known as Seneca the younger, or most commonly, simply Seneca. He was a statesman, philosopher, and playwright. His father was Seneca the elder, who was a prolific writer. He was exiled at one point in his life, only to return and be a mentor for the future emperor Nero.

In the year 54, when Nero eventually did become emperor, he became his advisor. He helped to create a competent world, but eventually, he started to lose influence over Nero. He eventually committed suicide after being accused for attempting to assassinate Nero. He was noted for having a rather calm suicide as well, often depicted in paintings.

He is most known for his writings, which often quote and pull things from other great stoics as well. He was incredibly resilient in his ability to endure certain things, and he will always be one of the most quoted stoics.

Musonius Rufus

He was a stoic teacher and writer. In fact, he was the teacher to the next philosopher on the list, Epictetus. He was a great teacher, up until the death of Seneca, in which Musonius was exiled as well. He still taught, but was no longer able to in the actual birthplace of stoicism, and instead did so in exile, away from Athens. Eventually, he did return to Rome, only to be banished once again by all philosophers.

He was most noted for discussing how stoics would be able to rise above all that was evil, including death. It wasn't that death was unavoidable, rather, stoic principles could help us to start fearing this idea much less.

Epictetus of Hierapolis

He was a philosopher as well as a pupil of Musonius Rufus. He is known for embracing life and all of its challenges, because he knew that we had to make the best with what we could. For everything else, it was best if we could take it as it occurs. The most astonishing thing about him isn't his origin story, but the fact that he never wrote anything down! It was his students that kept track of the knowledge he had to bestow onto others.

Originally a slave, his name actually means "acquired." That is what separates stoicism from a lot of other philosophies and even sciences of the time. anyone was a stoic, even Epictetus, who was born a slave. His real name is actually something that is still unknown.

Marcus Aurelius

He was the roman emperor from 161-180 AD. Marcus Aurelius was the last great emperor of ancient Rome and had a great passion for stoicism.

Power wasn't something he sought out, rather, something that had fallen into his possession. He was such a great stoic leader because he was humble and fair.

Though he could have anything he wanted as a man with such power, he never lived beyond his means and knew that there was no point in being overly excessive, an important idea we'll discuss later.

Chapter 4

The Distinction Between the Two Types of Virtue

Your virtuousness is like your righteousness. A virtue is something that makes up your morality, ethicalness, and spirit. Some would even describe a virtue as the state of your character. All virtue is different among each individual. Since there are so many factors that can go into defining virtue, there are no two that are alike. Even in certain friend groups or tight-knit families, when it comes down to it, we all react differently among various scenarios.

All of our interpersonal virtues differ as well, but when you have one, you have them all. It is the situation that calls upon the use of your virtue that will help define what it is that makes up that part of your character. Our variant experiences will sharpen these virtues, but the more defined one is, the better others will as well.

Plato split our virtues into four sections, Aristotle elaborated to twelve. Most philosophes generally still stick to these four categories. The four virtues that you need in order to live a good life include:

- Prudence
- Justice
- Fortitude
- Temperance

The translations can be a bit murky, so these are loosely divided into categories, but most virtues will follow under one of these four categories. (Plato, 380 BC)

Prudence is wisdom. How prepared are you for the future? What knowledge do you use in regard to your actions? How you gain and use this knowledge is going to be dependent on your virtue as well. Some individuals choose to ignore learning anything new, so they are lacking wisdom, knowledge, and prudence.

Justice is next. This is inclusive of what deserves respect and reward. Justice is not something that is simply measured on an individual level either. It is what is healthiest for the community. What best serves all people, not just some people. Some think emotion should be left out of justice, others believe you can't have these civic strengths without empathy involved. Your virtues around justice are dependent on your intellect and practicality with the subject.

Fortitude represents bravery. This is more dependent on your emotional strengths. What are you able to accomplish without fear? What can be achieved when no other emotional strains are holding you back.

Do you persevere through the challenging parts or turn away when faced with an obstacle? The level with which one seeks adventure and excitement lies within their fortuitous virtue.

Temperance is the moderation representation. How self-disciplined can you be? What, to you, is strong willpower? Those that are lacking in this virtue live in excess, detached from the realistic struggles and civic duties of those around them.

What is infrequently recognized within this virtue is forgiveness, both with others and with one's self. Revenge can lie within justice, but as you begin to connect these virtues, it is clear to see a low temperance level will make them more likely to be vengeful to fulfill interpersonal desires.

To live as a stoic, you must understand that these virtues can fall, or split, into two different categories, intellectual and practical virtue. To understand the difference means you will be better equipped to practice the sharpening of virtues overtime. Before knowing the difference, you must also accept that there will be no moment soon when you will be virtuous. It is a skill that grows overtime.

Seeking out these virtues isn't necessarily stoic either. Instead, they are what is gained on our path to becoming virtuous. You do not become virtuous and then become happy. Stoicism is about finding happiness along the path of increasing virtue.

Very few will become perfectly virtuous, but as time goes on, they will be able to be more aligned with strong virtuous ideas.

Intellectual Virtue

Our intellectual virtues are ones that help us to continually grow. Once you start to become an intellectual person, it's hard to go back. At first, others might think that you are annoying, always offering sage advice. As time goes on, you start to realize that others won't always learn from what you're trying to give them, and instead, have to come to these conclusions on their own.

This is where the double-edged sword of intellectuality can come into play. To build this virtue, you have to be curious, seek new experiences, and be patient with others around you that might be exploring virtue in other ways, at different paces.

Prudence is the first intellectual virtue. It can be hard to seek out learning in our teen years, or while in public schooling. Sometimes it comes after we are removed from educational institutions that learning can really become a passion. Others will choose to take leaving school as a reason to stop learning, but a stoic will accept this new-found freedom and take control of the continual knowledge they will choose to include in their lives.

Never underappreciate our ability to learn. When an opportunity arises to discover something new, whether it's about the world or yourself, accept this. Take in everything you can around you that can help you better understand the things that are occurring in our world.

Be curious, creative, critical in the way you think, and subjective in the manner you choose to judge. Always look for new skills to learn, and never cut yourself off from taking in new information.

Justice will be involved with your levels of empathy. Always put yourself in other people's shoes. Go through their lives when making judgements and ask not if you would do the same, but if what they did was appropriate depending on their current situation.

Do not seek revenge, as you shouldn't go against nature. A stoic will not seek punishment, they will find a way that they can help the other person grow, therefore expanding and solidifying their own intellectual virtue.

Integrity is another important branch of this intellectual virtue. Always do what you say you will do. Do not say you will do something you know you will not do. These seem like simple virtues, but not everyone is aware that they can be conscious of this kind of behavior.

Humility is an intellectual virtue that is also important. Be a friend to others or not, never an enemy.

Do not hate others, love them for their flaws and understand that they are humans. Be nursing, caring, generous, and loving. You can never be too kind, no matter how much you might want to be angry at the other person. To act as them is to be them, and that will only hurt your virtue.

At the end of the day, it will be your intellectual virtue that will still be dependent on your practical ones. The more you practice your virtue, the higher your intellectual levels will be.

Expertise and Time

These require expertise to build because you have to go through certain experiences to understand various life lessons. Though you can look to others and learn from their mistakes or actions, there are still some lessons you can only understand by actually going through them. For example, you can imagine what it would be like to lose a loved one, but when you actually experience this, it will be unlike anything you could have imagined.

As you get older, you will come to more realizations as well. We look to the future and hope for certain things or imagine life in various scenarios. It is only when we get there, when we become a certain age, that we fully understand what it means to be in that situation.

There are only certain things that you can get from passed time.

Not everything of value happens quickly. This can be what is most challenging in our current society. We demand things as quickly as possible, suffering through the waiting period. It is only after that period that we sometimes realize waiting was the best part of it all.

Practical Virtue

Prudence is the first intellectual virtue but is also a practical one. Wisdom and knowledge are so broad that it's how they are applied which determines if they are intellectual or practical. Your perspective is something that is already in existence, and there is no going back. You can change your perspective, but still on a scale based on what you believed in the first place.

Temperance is also a practical virtue. How you make decisions and the factors that drive your choices can be what helps you determine your virtuous temperance.

Your fortitude, rather, bravery, will be another practical virtue. Many of us are defined by our past experiences when it comes to how courageous we might be in any given scenario.

It is practical when it is involved with crafting and skillful abilities. Any form of art or creation, of that matter, can require productive elements which would qualify themselves as a practical virtue.

Result of Habit

Our virtues aren't based in something that happens just once. It is a collection of all of our experiences, thus, reminding us that they result as a form of habit. Our virtues can become weakened by certain habits we do, however.

When you fall into a place of repeated thinking, you start to think that it is true. It becomes your reality.

Our practical virtues are ones that are developed from habits. In order to live a virtuous life, we have to recognize our habits, the practical virtues they have created, and whether these are correct, or in accordance with nature.

Where you went to school, how you grew up, these are all going to help shape your courageousness, your willpower. One pattern of thinking you might have had is that those who are poor are that way because they don't work hard enough. This is an idea that can be taught and created based on perception.

When you believe this, you lack virtue that is based in humility and prudence, which can affect your generosity and empathy.

A virtuous stoic would understand that some people might be poor because they don't work hard, but for many, there are various socioeconomic factors that can play a role in determining one's status.

This virtue can be based in practicality, what was taught and shaped as a result of education and society. It can be altered and improved through intellectual virtue so that this stoic can become virtuous in humility, justice, and prudence.

How to Recognize the Distinction

Self-reflection is going to be the way to recognize this distinction. You have to constantly ask yourself what it was that made you think that way. When a thought pops into your head, especially a definitive one that makes a judgement, it's important to look internally for the reason behind that thought.

When you start to make assumptions and create your morals, ask if that is the best way something can be formed. Is this virtue based in intellectuality, or is it rather a result of habit? Only then will you know whether or not you can find a place of preferred indifference with the virtue to align your believes in accordance with nature.

When you are self-reflecting, you should use the four distinctions as what you will determine your own virtues on.

You do not need to have a strict limitation on which values you care to be truer. Some are interested in bravery, others would rather focus on wisdom. Both can be stoic. Remember that as you define these virtues, the others will become naturally sharpened as well. To be virtuous is to be highly skilled in all levels, something to remember.

You will then have to recognize the distinction further by deciding if it's something that is practical or intellectual.

This is important to know because both will be treated differently when trying to interpersonally grow. Intellectual will be things that you should try to flourish. How can you become more knowledgeable, stronger-willed, and accepting of others? When you stop being intellectual, you can stop growing fairly quickly.

Your practical virtues are ones that you will want to focus on questioning. There will be more confrontation. You have to face yourself and figure out what is the seed of this thought? Was it something that you were taught to believe, or is it an idea you formed on your own? Is it based in logic or rather something cultivated by emotion?

When I Started Practicing this Distinction

As I faced more confrontations in my life, I started to question what I might be doing wrong that required me to be punished. When I would get a flat tire, have a nasty cold, or miss the bus, I would think, "why me?"

I didn't want this person to be my character anymore. Now, I place an emphasis on taking these challenges as a test of my virtue.

I would look at the things I went through and find something that could help me grow. I became tired of always thinking that everything in my life was terrible, and my efforts to find a challenge-free life were futile. Instead, I started to realize that it was better for me to seek out a way of thinking that was grounded in accepting everything for what it is.

I focus on the distinction to decide if it is something that is habit that I need to challenge, or whether I have not yet faced a lesson to be learned.

For example, let's look at the small challenge of getting your car towed (something I don't like to admit has happened to me more than once). This can easily be a time where you want to give up, cry, scream, and become angry. This is how I felt the first time it happened to me.

I thought of everything I could have done wrong and what I should have done, causing me to agonize even after I got my car back and paid the fees. The second time it happened, I realized that all of this was pointless. I didn't learn my lesson because I was too busy thinking about how horrible my life was. The second time around, I recognized that it wasn't the end of the world, that I needed this in my life to make me more responsible and aware of my surroundings.

I accepted the discomfort and used it to grow rather than something that validated my negative perspective like it had the first time.

Stoicism is on such a broader scale that we shouldn't always look at these specified smaller instances or else we'll go crazy. Not everything that happens in your life has to be a philosophical experience, some things will simply be a matter of chance.

However, for explanatory purposes, I'll be using smaller examples throughout the book. Always look at the big picture and remember that not everything that happens is a "sign." Though, if that is something you believe, that is fine too! Not everything has to have meaning, but if you look hard enough, it certainly will.

Living in Maintained Control

"When forced, as it seems, by circumstances into utter confusion, get a hold of yourself quickly. Don't be locked out of the rhythm any longer than necessary.

You'll be able to keep the beat if you are constantly returning to it." – Marcus Aurelius (Aurelius, 180 AD)

Understanding the distinction of these virtues, how to control and monitor them, and how to develop them further is important, because really, that'swhat philosophy is all about.

Life isn't about living from one circumstance to the next. Instead, you should be taking it all in at once, using everything at your disposal to question, define, and sharpen your virtues.

From a stoic point of view, things aren't going to be all about what's waiting for you once you've mastered your virtues. Instead, it is a focus on how you can continually define, sculpt, and clean-up your virtues. You shouldn't worry about becoming virtuous so that you get a "reward," such as happiness. Your journey should be to discover happiness while you are going through these experiences that help to cultivate your virtue.

Those that Lack Virtue

Condemning others for lacking virtue is a waste of time because they are already punishing themselves by their behavior. As I said before, the double-edged sword is that you either get cast off or ignored when sharing virtuous thoughts, or you are lonely within your own beliefs. Don't let yourself fall into either side of this and live in a place where you are focused on yourself and growing from within, not trying to change others. Many will learn better by example rather than condemnation anyway.

Chapter Recap:

- Your virtue is your morality, and the values that you believe in. It is created by your past and present and is based on how you plan to live in the future as well. Virtue isn't what we want to achieve, but something that we might already have that we need to expand on.

- Your intellectual virtue is what you need to perfect overtime. There are some things that can only be learned through age and experience.

- Your practical virtue is what has resulted because of habit. The environment you were raised in counts towards your level of virtue, and whether you choose to keep or lose habits will also be important in defining virtue.

Chapter 5
Eliminating Absolute Self-Talk

When we use phrases like "always," "never," "everyone," "nobody," we are automatically making absurd conclusions. These are terms used in one singular moment that define multiple instances we aren't logically comparing. Talk like this can inflate situations and create false perspectives. When you are continually defining your life in absolutes, things will easily become "either or," "this or that," and other polarized thinking that can lead to unhappy thoughts and negative perspectives. We need to reduce this kind of thinking (Reinalda, 2014).

We absolute self-talk for a few reasons. First, because it makes a more interesting story. If I said, "today wasn't a good day," you would shrug it off and think it was no big deal. If I said, "today was the worst day of my life," you would perk up and wait to hear about what happened that made it so bad.

We like to use this kind of phrasing because it will help keep people more interested. You also likely will be more engaged with what I have to say if I make sure to tell a riveting story, meaning that I will be gratified with a higher level of attention given from someone else. To be stoic is to not seek out this extra attention because it is not needed.

Others will eventually start to take interest in your stories because of the honesty, and your ability to pull important ideas from simple instances rather than inflating something small to create a false idea.

Absolute self-talk is also a way that we can identify things. As humans, we are consistently trying to label things. This is another reason that we will uses phrases like, "always," or "every time." It is hard to navigate through the world because we run into so much that we don't understand.

Even looking at your computer, phone, tablet, or whatever else you're reading from now can be hard. You understand how it turns on, how to get to the things you want and need, and how to charge it when the battery runs low. How well do you fully understand it, however? There are so many things we run into in this world we don't understand, and might not ever, but our brains aren't satisfied with that idea. It's in our animalistic nature to try and figure things out.

This is our way of determining if something is a threat, helpful, useful, or a waste. Do we need this information, or do we not? It's either good or bad, no in between. Absolutes will help us categorize things we come in contact with. If you hate bananas, then you might think you hate everything that has a banana in it, even though many of these types of foods can actually taste very different from each other.

We don't just speak in absolute with the phrases mentioned in the first sentence of this section either. We also categorize absolutes.

In terms of gender, many people find confusion with anyone that doesn't present themselves either wholly masculine or feminine, because that means other typical labels might be confused as well. We do this with religion, race, sexual orientation, and many other factors that we use to distinguish identity as well. Certain groups might seem more dangerous, weak, sinful, good, or bad than others based in perspectives we have that have been cultivated by our society. This kind of thinking leads to a black/white perspective where we fail to see the truths that lie within the gray area.

If we can eliminate absolute self-talk, we will strengthen our perspectives.

It doesn't mean that we believe in what we are accepting of, rather, we take it as it is on a separate level, not trying to define it one way or another. You don't have to believe in the philosophies of an opposing religion, but you have to understand that those that do aren't to be labeled in any certain way based on the absolute assumptions gathered from others who are similar.

When you start to use these absolute phrases, you eliminate the chance to be prudent. You see a thief on the local news and think that they are a bad person.

In doing this, the reality that they were trying to feed their family is lost, making the bigger picture obsolete, keeping the chance to strengthen your virtue away.

Absolute Phrases

When we use too many absolute phrases, it could even lead to polarized thinking. When you are thinking like this, you aren't giving yourself the chance to really see all possibilities. A reason that others have for avoiding neutral thinking is because we don't think we can be impartial!

You might think you either have to fully believe in something or completely deny it. Our society isn't as accepting of things that lie in between one point or another because it is harder to label it. A stoic is not afraid of something that lacks labels, rather, they seek this mystery out.

Our brain tries to take so many short-cuts, which is why we will use an absolute. You might think you're starving when you're just as hungry as every other day, because your brain is creating the urgency to get you to eat. We aren't always at fault for the absolutes created.

Oftentimes, it is the simple chemistry of our animalistic brains.

You have to start recognizing when you say these so that you can really challenge your perspective. You don't have to live on one end or the other. Instead, you should aim to balance somewhere in the middle, not believing in either side, but accepting the realities of both.

If we speak in absolute phrases too much, we will blur our perceptions and make it more difficult to change our views, our

virtues. These give us a sense of security, but all great stoics know that we should be seeking the discomfort. To do that, avoid using these phrases.

Absolute phrases also cause you to summarize what other people might be saying, which could lead to you jumping to conclusions. A person might be using absolutes, and then you categorize their thoughts based on those, when really, they're just using these phrases to exaggerate their stories. Do your best to limit the number of absolutes that you allow into your speech and thinking patterns.

Always, Never, Ever, Anytime

These phrases pop up way too often. We say things like, "I'm always on time," "I'm never this slow," "This is the worst to ever exist," "It rains anytime I go outside." This kind of thinking starts to define time.

What your brain does when you say things like this is to search through itself to look for times to validate this kind of thinking.

If someone thinks, "my boyfriend never does anything nice for me," they will then start to imagine all of the times that they felt similar, and the moments where he might have been mean. A brain not aware of these absolutes can start to think this is true, ignoring all of the good that has actually been done.

These are damaging because they might sound like you are making accusations if using them in language with others. Saying things like, "you always do this," can be hurtful to someone else, and makes them feel as though they are consistently a bad person.

They will also blur your perception of time, generalizing it too much. If it rained four days in a row, you might think, "I hate it here, it's always raining," even though it's only rained 4/30 days that month. Instead, we need to look at the realistic situation and use better phrasing that doesn't make harsh definitions.

Use often, rarely, currently, or sometimes. You should always aim to talk just about the current situation, as a stoic knows that the "now" is what is most important. However, there are some situations where you might still need to use certain words, and absolutes should be your last choice.

Best and Worst or First and Last

These phrases can be challenging because they create limitations. "This is the best day of my life," "It was the ultimate Christmas present," these are absolutes that come as natural feelings but should be used cautiously.

It is not bad to feel that particular way, but with that definition, we can become disappointed when other things don't compare.

We should also be weary of ranking things. You might be better at things, but not the best. Ranking can become too definitive. Instead of accepting things for what they are, we judge them based on their good and bad qualities. We shouldn't take something in based on a certain scale. When it comes to bigger things in life, whether it's a friend, a job, an idea, or even the food we eat, we can't judge it based on predisposed matched criteria. We should accept things for what they are.

When you create a scale, that sets stopping points. Stoics know that you need to not do this, but instead know that upward progression is always going to be the best way to go. If you say, "this is the last day I'm going to eat unhealthy," it can be hard to follow through with a weight loss plan. Instead, you should be accepting of reality, which means that including a few days a month to eat unhealthy can actually help keep a diet on track.

The same thinking goes with first or last. You're putting time limitations on different events in your life.

Don't define your future with an absolute that we want to use in the moment. You never know where your life might end up in a year, five years, or a decade down the line.

Even thinking, "I hope this is the last time I'm at the hospital," could end up coming back to disappoint you. Obviously we want to avoid the hospital at all costs, because it means perfect health. To imagine decades into the future of ourselves, as well as our spouses, children, or closest friends never needing to go to the hospital is foolish. We don't have to live in fear of it, but instead, we should be accepting the hospital for what it is.

Though it is not the ideal place to be, it is still nice to know that in the future, should something happen to our health or the conditions of a loved one, we have a place like a hospital to go to. A stoic won't try to change their thinking to believe that hospitals are great, fun places to be. That's unrealistic. They will, however, look for the benefits that hospitals bring, and how they help societies function.

Can't, Won't, Shouldn't, and Wouldn't

Anything that you might use "not" after could potentially limit your actions. We're often told that we should never say that we can't do something, but we often forget how important this truly is. When you limit what you are able to do, you are limiting your potential growth.

We use these kinds of phrases as a summary for other reasons when we might feel we are unable to do something. Whenever you allow yourself to say or think like this, always ask why.

There are usually multiple reasons that you will discover. Sometimes, the same thing will be true based on your findings, but it's important that we're still digging deep to uncover the potential reasons as to why we are making these assumptions. Often you'll find that we jumped to that absolute premeditatively and should have really questioned ourselves before making that decision. This is because we are usually deciding for our future selves when we say things like "can't," or "won't."

"I can't go back to college." Are you sure? Or is it that you just don't want to? Going back to school is something that is risky because it costs money, takes time, and could lead to a different life, which is simply scary.

It's easy to look at these on the surface level and think there's no way you could make that decision, but when you dive deeper into those areas, you realize that it's all actually very feasible. Whether or not it is the right decision, if it is in accordance with nature, will be up to you, but by eliminating the absolute self-talk, you are opening more avenues of discovery.

You can dive deeper into yourself and your true desires, figuring out the reality of situations that you have been preemptively labeling too often in the past.

Nothing, Everything, Definitely

These are the terms that are probably the most absolute, besides "absolute" itself. As we mentioned in the introduction, stoicism can sometimes be perceived as a sort of reaction to nihilism.

It is the answer to the question itself, what is the point? When you become a stoic, you start to define "the point." You discover reasons for going on, meaning behind things that you would have blown off otherwise, and answers to some of the most intellectually challenging questions you faced.

"Nothing matters," is a common phrase you'll hear among many that deem themselves intellectually. To come to this realization is nothing philosophical itself. It is the truth. Nothing does matter, because life will continue to go on. Even when faced with the worst disaster.

There will always be movement after, so it can be easy to fall into this thought pattern. Stoicism then comes in and says, "some things matter based in virtue, and what matters is created by us and our experiences throughout our lives."

If you are using "nothing" or "everything," you are dumping so much complexity into one group. You are ignoring everything that makes things interesting, specialized, different, important.

When you see a terrible news story, it can be easy to think that there is nothing good in life. You might hear about a horrible tragedy and think that everything is terrible.

We all fall into this kind of mentality at one point on our journey to stoicism. What we start to realize, however, is that this is a false assumption. While there might be five news stories a night about death and disaster, there will always be at least one good one. That tragedy itself can also help to show us the good, whether it's the way people come together to heal after such catastrophe, or if it's the empathetic response that reminds us not "everything" is terrible.

When speaking, remember that people are going to respond more to your realistic verbatim than something that seems overdone. "It's difficult to think of something greater than the sound of a child's laugh," is more effective than, "nothing is better than children laughing." We hear the "nothing is better than," and ignore it.

When you say, "it's difficult to think of," that gets others thinking of things that would be better.

As a stoic, you are going to be making it your goal to get others talking. Saying "Everything in my life is going great right now," you sound more off-putting than a humbler, "I'm appreciative to say that not many things are going wrong in my life."

Both can have the same meaning, but one sounds more open to discussion than the other, and a realistic portrayal rather than a fabricated fantasy.

How This Strategy Changes Your Perception

Not only will it help how others see you, but how you might perceive others. After years of absolute self-talk, you can start to fall into a thinking pattern where everything is one or the other.

This can cause anger, confusion, frustration, and depression. One that thinks everything is either good or bad will fail to see the things that fall in between. They limit their perspective, which ultimately limits their growth potential.

When we start reflecting in ourselves, it becomes easier to see that in other people. When we realize the way that we have always thought before doesn't have to be our pattern of thinking going forward, it is very freeing.

Understanding that we can be accepting of that which we don't understand and open to new things we would have otherwise cast off is like starting a new life. rather than pushing things to one side or the other, we can accept them at face value, for what they are, not creating a potentially damaging perspective.

What it's Like Before you Recognized This

You likely didn't even realize that you were doing it before this. It's the way that many people talk. Before you realize how this can change your perception, you likely often felt confused about your beliefs, maybe to the point that you were even anxious in defining them.

When we talk in absolutes, we think that we have to have all the answers now. It can feel confusing and pressuring to try to know it all now. When you realize that everything should be accepted as it is, then it becomes much easier to live in accordance with nature.

We don't realize how effective this polarized thinking can be, however. It might even change the way that other people see us. Though we might only use absolutes as a way of telling a story, it can make others think that we have different kinds of perspectives when it comes to the tales we tell.

Absolutes create expectations, which many great stoics have stated are far too high. When you use absolutes, it creates images in your head. "The worst bathroom in the country," is far more frightening than, "a gross bathroom."

Lowered expectations isn't meant to sound disappointing or depressing.

It's not that we shouldn't still have expectations. We just need to make sure they are realistic, in accordance with nature.

"This is my last day ever working for a company I hate," is a great feeling when we're in the final stretch of transitioning from one job to another. However, we are prophesying that the job we're going to is going to be the one that we end up in. That might be the plan, but as a stoic, we need to be realistic and understand anything could happen, including you having to go back to a job you dislike.

This isn't to create fear, but instead, a way to take care of our future selves and make sure that we are leaving all avenues open, not defining the way things should be. How can we ever know where life will be in a year? When things don't go as we planned, it starts to create panic. You imagine that you are doing something wrong because you're not in a place that you imagined you would be. This is an unfair expectation to put on ourselves. Instead, we have to remember to always accept things for what they are.

How Things are Better Now as a Result of Practicing

When you accept the gray area, it won't be so scary to be right in the middle of it. I used to believe that to be a strong person, you had to have strong morals. I still believe that, however, having strong morals doesn't mean putting things into strict categories.

I would think that if something were true in one situation, it was true in all situations.

I thought I had to treat everyone the exact same way in all situations, rather than doing so on a situational basis. I was creating labels for myself every day, trying to categorize more and more, realizing that it was too hard to keep up with my idealizations and expectations after a while.

When I stopped letting absolutes into my vocabulary and thought process, I saw almost immediate change.

You will notice your perspective broadening when you drop labels and absolutes and focus on reality instead. Rather than trying to define who I was, I accepted myself for what I am now. I am not perfect, and I have flaws, but these are important in defining my character. Everything about me is different from anyone else because of my experiences.

I know that we are all different, and the worst thing I can do now is to try and label something or create clear definitions. The more accepting of the future I am and prepared for things to go in different ways than I imagined, the easier it is to remain in the present and be appreciative of the "now."

There are still going to be moments that you are saying, "this is the best taco I've ever had," and things such as that, but you should understand the reality behind these phrases. You aren't at fault for these absolutes. They will still come up. Just ensure they are only "story" tactics, and not things that are actually defining the way you believe.

Living in Maintained Control

I can live in maintained control because of this now as it has forced me into contemplation. When I say, "this was the worst day," I stop myself.

I think of all the other times that were challenging and remembered that going through the challenging experiences I might have that day were only there to make me stronger. I look at a bad day and am appreciative that it wasn't any worse than it was, or else I would feel a lot more terrible at the end of the day.

Once I question, "is this really happening always?" I have to look back on time. I might think, "my friend is always using me," when I feel like I'm getting taken advantage of, but then I recognize that it was an absolute and I need to question that reality rather than validating it. I look back at all the times my friend has helped me out, and I remember that they would do the same in my scenario.

It has forced me to question my standards as well. When I say best/worst, or if I start to rank things, I question if I should be putting them on a scale in the first place. It has helped me to control my emotional reactions and the way that I perceive things because I no longer try to label things on a certain spectrum.

Chapter 6

Do and Feel What is Appropriate in Every Circumstance

"Your happiness depends on three things, all of which are within your power: your will, your ideas concerning the events in which you are involved, and the use you make of your ideas." – Epictetus (Epictetus, 1595)

There are a lot of things in life that seem unfair. Certain things are out of our control, and we struggle to comprehend things that don't fully make sense. We try to come up with definitions, rules, and restrictions, that we form into morals. We judge ourselves and each other on our own morality. What we have to shift to instead, however, is increasing our virtue.

When we are too dependent on coming up with strict patterns for our own behavior, then we can end up falling into a place where we lose sight of what is actually important. A huge part of stoic philosophy is the act of doing what is appropriate in every circumstance. We can't try and change things to be our way, and we can't run when something doesn't go as we thought it would. We can't predict how we are going to feel, and we won't always be prepared for some of the things that get thrown at us.

What we have to focus on doing more than anything, the thing that is most important to us, is to feeling what is appropriate, and doing what we think is based on that circumstance. If you give yourself too many rules and define yourself based on strict morals, then it can be hard to see what is actually best in a certain situation. Instead, you might find that you become too focused on fulfilling an ideal you have made from presumptions rather than doing what is right in that circumstance.

If you were born with certain disadvantages, then there are inequalities that exist in our world which hold others back. There will always be things that will be out of our control, in that way.

We can't change how others see us, no matter what we might try and do. It is up to us to be ourselves, be true to who we are, and act accordingly to the circumstance, not anything else. We can spend hours wishing for another life, get lost in fantasy, and even take risky action to try and get the things that we want, but a stoic knows that they have to take their situation and make the most out of it.

Sometimes, we have to just work with what we have. Simply trying your hardest is the only thing that you can do. Being a stoic is all about learning what is and isn't in your control. This can be the hard distinction to find. Sometimes, our brains will naturally come up with what we think are solutions to help us out of a certain scenario.

We get anxious and start to predict what might happen in the future, and what terrible thing is going to occur that we'll have to deal with.

What we have to understand, however, is that it's time to accept the situation for what it is. No matter how hard we try, or how badly we want to, there are many situations that will simply be out of our control.

Do what is appropriate in every circumstance. We will get into how to do this in the next section, but it's first important to understand what makes up your circumstance. When self-reflecting, it can be easy to see the negative parts of our life. that is what we are trained to do, because our brains are dependent on survival.

Your circumstance can seem a certain way to you, but completely opposite to someone else. While you might be miserable, someone else might be envious that you have fewer issues than them. It's really just a matter of both perspectives, as everyone has good and bad parts to their life.

When looking at your circumstance, judge it objectively, as it is. How would you describe it to another person? What would you say if you were writing your biography? What would the character description be of you if you were in a movie? You are not wrong for forming your perspective but remember that your circumstance is separate from what you might be perceiving. Trust what you feel as well.

When we become too oriented in purpose, intent, outcome, and risk, we can sometimes get lost.

Your intuition, your gut feeling, these all are things that can help drive decision. Some individuals will think that this is a reckless perspective, but you also have to remember that sometimes, it is our natural instincts telling us what is best.

Trusting what you feel is also risky because it can also be a perspective wedged in emotion. You might feel you're doing what is right, but it could be to serve an emotional purpose you aren't fully aware of. Still, intuition is important in defining so that we can better judge scenarios as they come to us.

Judging What is Suitable

The situation doesn't change based on your circumstance. Just because you want something to change and are hoping for a better future doesn't mean that it's going to happen. Instead, you need to make sure that you are taking action to change the scenario within your boundaries and learning how to accept the things that will always be true.

For example, if you hate your apartment but can't afford something nicer, you can change your job to try and make more money. However, you are only going to be able to make so much more money, so you will also have to find a way to be happy with what you already have in the meantime, while you save up or look for something nicer.

Though you might be able to get out of there eventually, in that circumstance, you have to accept what you have and let it motivate you for the future.

Embrace the struggle, because when you get the thing that you desire, you will appreciate it much more. To first do this, you have to

look at what is in and out of your control. Back to the apartment example, when hunting, rent prices are going to be out of your control. You might find a landlord you can negotiate with, but you won't be able to get an $800 apartment for $400. This is something that you can't control. However, you can control your judgements. If you want a place with a jacuzzi tub, but you only have a few hundred a month, you're not going to find that. This is what you can change, your perspective on the tub.

No matter who you are in life, you have circumstances that are specific to you, and based on those, you judge what is suitable to your life. It can be hard to see that another person is living in a nicer apartment than you, especially if it's someone your age, or even in the same career path. What you have to remember, however, is that you cannot change your situation to be like theirs, and you can only do what you can to help improve the one you're in, no matter the pace.

To do this, you have to remember that every circumstance is different. Though that person might be living in a nicer apartment, maybe they are in far worse debt.

Perhaps they have a parental figure or spouse that pays for the apartment, but maybe they have a bad relationship with this person that is draining them emotionally.

They might not even realize how lucky they are to have the nice apartment, but as a person that has struggled in a place they don't like, you have learned to be appreciative. You have grown your virtue, and they have stayed the same, and for that, you should be appreciative as it is. Both circumstances are different, so you can only make judgements based in your own situation.

As a stoic, you can start to change your perspective about your situation much easier when you understand which circumstances surround you. When we consistently agonize over the things that are out of our control, it can make everything else feel so much worse. A healthier perspective that will do more for us in the long run is to learn how to sit with the discomfort. Find a way to be happy, appreciative, or content with the things that you have been given.

When it comes to taking action, it's important to remember that we have to do what feels right.

It can be hard to do this, because we get so hung up on the "what ifs."

Remember that it is more important to make the wrong decision, then to never make one at all. A decision is a decision.

You have to understand that there are no mistakes or accidents. They are just detouring in the road down a long path to the Good Life. Even if what you do ends up having consequences it is still something that has become a learning experience. Rather than wasting time trying to figure out what we should do or looking back on the past and holding onto regret, we have to focus on doing what is right and moving forward.

Accepting Circumstance Becomes Easier

When you start to do the best with what you have, it is easier to see the greatness that surrounds you. It's not that happiness is a choice. This is something that many people misunderstand. It's rather that our judgements around a scenario are a choice, and the more we place judgement on expanding our virtues, the happier we can become.

There will always be moments where you still think, "that's not fair," but remember, someone else might be thinking the same situation about you. When you aren't sure what to do, or don't know if you're making the right decision based in virtue, remember that you simply must do what feels right.

Even if it's scary, hard, or goes against what other people think is best for you, ultimately, it's up to you to do what feels right.

There might be consequences, but that becomes part of accepting the circumstance. Even if there are negative outcomes, we can still take these in as learning experiences that help us grow to be greater than we imagined.

What it's Like Before you Recognized This

Before we recognize that situations do not change just because of how we feel, the world seems very fair and unbalanced. Rather than looking at the things that we can change and doing so, we get stuck on the things that we can't and become comfortable in our unhappiness.

The people that realize that they can change certain things and overcome the challenges that used to hold them back are the people that will find the most success. There are certainly things that seem unfair that have been given to us in this life. it would be great if we were all born perfectly healthy to rich parents, ensuring we wouldn't have to struggle or work that hard.

However, this isn't the case, and there are some circumstances that will hold others back a little more. It's not about pretending like we all have equal opportunities.

A stoic recognizes the different struggles that we have been presented. The emphasis for stoics is to seek the things they can change, and to make the best they can of that in the direction of something better.

It limits your perspective when you fail to have perspective on your circumstances. When you feel as though everything is out of your control, then that becomes reality. When you start to have the perspective that day after day, everything is someone else's fault, then nothing will ever change. It is up to you to realize the things within your control.

At the same time, we also can't pretend that anything is possible. Many things are possible but saying "anything" is an absolute that can make it hard to do or feel what is right in any circumstance.

How Things are Better Now as a Result of Practicing

When we can start separating our actions based on our circumstances, then it will be easier to stop comparing ourselves to others. It is easier to leave behind the thoughts of wanting something greater or wishing that things would suddenly change.

Some will find themselves living only from one happy circumstance to the next, trying to deny all the pain they feel in between. A stoic accepts the suffering and uses it to grow. It is something that can become a driver in your pursuit of knowledge.

We will always have challenges in our life, things we wish we did differently, and fears about the future. We have to keep ourselves grounded in those situations and do what is best for those circumstances.

You will be able to much more easily pull the beauty out of what you used to see as a burden. This can be very enlightening for the most angered souls. When you feel as though everything is terrible, then it's time to start to look at things that are great. Someone depressed, lonely, and hated by many can also be someone completely healthy surrounded by wealth.

Another person that is stricken with multiple illnesses in debt can also be completely happy. The only thing that can really give us happiness is virtue, and that will be grown by doing what we can in all situations. Making the most of what we have and doing what we think is right is the only thing we can really do to ensure happiness.

When I Started Practicing This

"Caretake this moment. Immerse yourself in its particulars. Respond to this person, this challenge, this deed. Quit the evasions. Stop giving yourself needless trouble. It is time to really live; to fully inhabit the situation you happen to be in now. You are not some disinterested bystander. Participate. Exert yourself." – Epictetus (Epictetus, 1595)

I've had certain challenges based on the demographic that I was born into.

Things out of my control have led to judgement from others that caused me to question my worth and believe

I am "less than" because of other's preconceived notions of who I should be.

Seeing other people with privileges I wish I had was challenging. I would feel envious, jealous, and stricken with rage at some points because they had what I wanted. All the time that I was looking at others, I was too busy to see what I had around me.

I was feeling really terrible about myself for a period of time, wishing everything was different.

I would follow people on social media and see that they were living seemingly happier lives than me. It wasn't until someone I knew that had everything lost it all in a nasty divorce inflated from a secret addiction. I didn't envy a person, I envied an idea. They weren't a happy couple with loving people that I thought. They had their own struggles too, but they didn't share that, so I failed to see it. I was only looking at the perspective from my point of view. I wasn't looking at the actual circumstance.

We all go through things that are good, and some that are bad. We just have to do what's right, do what we can. The better you can make the most with what you have, the easier life will be, and the more virtuous you can become.

Living in Maintained Control

I have been able to live a happier life by doing this, in control of my emotions, because I know that there is no use in being angry over the things I was given I can't control. When I am upset, I ask if I can control it or not. When I can't, I remember to accept this reality and remind myself of other truths that create a positive perspective. When I can change something, then I do everything in my power, and accept that progress can take time.

I am filled with less envy, because I know that we are all just doing the best that we can. I don't look at others and wish for what they have. I see their individual beauty and appreciate their uniqueness, just as I do in myself.

The main thing to remember from this is that if we don't learn to just do what we can, we are wasting time! Anytime spent wishing for something different is time that could be spent actually doing what it takes to create a more desirable scenario.

Chapter 7

Only Your Judgement Makes Something Either Good or Bad

"Remember, it is not enough to be hit or insulted to be harmed, you must believe that you are being harmed. If someone succeeds in provoking you, realize that your mind is complicit in the provocation. Which is why it is essential that we not respond impulsively to impressions; take a moment before reacting, and you will find it easier to maintain control." – Epictetus (Epictetus, 1595)

This next chapter blends into the last one well, as your circumstance is going to be separate from your judgements on whether or not something is good or bad. This Epictetus quote helps to summarize this idea well, using a common occurrence as an example; the act of being hurt by someone else.

If someone punches you, it's going to hurt physically, but mentally, it will be for you to decide how to react. If a person insults you, they are at fault for saying something they shouldn't have, but they are not to blame if you take action, such as insulting them back or even using violence. This is important to remember.

If we mention someone getting under your skin, you probably have a person pop up in your head.

It can be easy to think that they are the enemy, they are annoying, or they are bad.

What we have to remember, however, is that this is not the truth whatsoever. We are only allowing that to be the truth because of our judgements.

We are placing them on a scale in our mind, matching their qualities to criteria we've created based on our experiences and teachings from society and educational institutions. You can change your thinking, whether it's on a person, a situation, an experience, or whatever else it is that you're judging. Only what you choose to believe, how you react and handle those emotional responses is what defines your judgement on whether something is good or bad.

Your perspective is based in your judgements, which are based in teachings. If someone makes an annoyed face at you, you can take that as them having a funny looking face, or you can decide that they are personally attacking you. The circumstance is the same, but whether you believe it to be good or bad is simply based in the judgement you have on that scenario.

The situation is going to be the same, but there are going to be many versions of how it felt emotionally from person to person. A stoic remains as objective as possible in order to not inflate or demonize the things they encounter.

It's not that you won't have a perspective

– you will understand all the perspectives.

This is the best way to help you properly find the best solution to any given circumstance.

Emotions are Based Upon a Judgement

Many have the misconception that stoics are lacking emotion. This is not true. They just attempt to separate themselves from emotion so that they can more properly react to the situation realistically. Humans are going to feel emotion, even those that seem the most lacking it. What differentiates in us all, however, is the way that we choose to react to an emotion. Someone can lash out when upset, or they can choose to sit quietly and work through their feelings.

Anger is simply our judgment about an event, and we can react to that anger with aggression, internalized rage, depression, an attempt at peace, and many more potential actions can be taken when someone feels angry. A stoic will separate themselves from that anger, question why it is there, and attempt to not let it drive them. Instead, they will study themselves and the scenario to improve on their virtue.

There are biological purposes to having emotions.

As a stoic, we should try and rewire our brains in order to make rational decisions based in reality. We don't have to separate ourselves from our

biology. It's not about suppressing that emotion. What we need to do is look to our biology for the answers.

What do we feel is being taken away, threatened, or desired? What natural urges are causing us to have this emotional reaction? What have we experienced in our past to help us form these judgements? Questioning these motives will help us to break apart our judgements, making it easier to perceive a bad situation as a good one.

This isn't to be pessimistic or optimistic. You don't need to change the way that you're thinking so that everything is good all the time. Some situations can be very challenging to find benefits from, so instead of seeing something as "good," we still have to accept things for what they are, and sometimes, that means sitting through discomfort or enduring pain to learn something meaningful that shapes our virtue.

The Enchiridion

"Men are not disturbed by things, but by the views which they take of things." - Epictetus (Epictetus, 125 AD)

The Enchiridion is also known as Handbook of Epictetus. It wasn't written by the stoic himself, but rather, a student, Arrian, that compiled the content. It dives into many parts of stoicism, a major one being the control of our judgments.

If you take judgment out of circumstances, then you are indifferent. They are not "good" or "bad" they just are. This is the state that a stoic should attempt to perceive all things. We can still enjoy moments that are good, and we might still experience pain in times that are bad, but it's important that we make sure to look at all circumstances for what they are.

Epictetus describes an internal world that is made up of things that we enjoy and dislike. These things can benefit us, but they can also cause harm. Not having them might cause pain, and we can experience challenging things in our attempt to get them.

Our freedom lies within the ability to choose how you will feel about a situation. We don't have the freedom to change all situations into something that we desire, but we do have the ability to change how we feel about that circumstance.

Another misconception some have about this stoic idea is that it's supposed to be easy. You can't just wake up one day and start to be happy about the things that were causing agony yesterday.

It's going to take time, and there will be moments where you feel completely hopeless for a future remotely better than what you're living in now. We have to remember that a stoic understands this is a lifelong journey. Defining virtue means being self-disciplined, and that can sometimes mean going against animalistic instincts.

This is a practice that will take time. It is not a race that you have to try and win. You won't have to worry about completing anything quickly. Instead, accept that each day will get better and better.

Emotions That Are Restricting Your Advancement

Emotions are good, they are relatable, and they remind us that we feel. We can't stop emotions from happening. We simply have to take them in as they are. We will never get to a place where we have removed the ability to feel emotion, and we shouldn't. That's not the goal of stoics. Instead, they know how to separate action from emotion so that all judgements are based in reality and our current circumstance.

Emotions should not dictate how we live our life. We will make many decisions based in emotion in our life, but we should do our best to try and be just and logical when defining our virtue.

If everything is based in anger, passion, love, anxiety, or some other emotion that has commonly driven you in the past, then you won't beable to properly decide whether you are making a judgement in reality or not.

Accept how you feel when confronted. Don't deny your feelings. Practice counting, breathing, and waiting before reacting. When someone angrily texts you, set the phone down. Whenever someone raises their voice, stay quiet, even just for a moment. You will start to realize that better outcomes occur when you wait and approach things with patience rather than trying to react right away on emotion. Even if it's dealing with an outside source, maybe a debt collector. It can feel like the end of the world, and emotions can take you to high places, but we have to look at the situation logically and remember that in order to advance, we have to be virtuous, both practically and intellectually.

This goes for positive emotions too, like excitement. You might have gotten a bonus from work but wait before you spend it on a night out over the weekend. The initial excitement you feel is good, but the excitement you feel from assurance and avoidance of disappointment will be better.

If you have to at first, avoid the situations that cause emotion. If you are constantly fighting with a friend, take a break.

Process the reality of the situation, reflect, and rejuvenate, and try to go back and mend the relationship when you have more of an awareness over your emotions.

We have to also become aware of the emotions we feel about ourselves, and who we actually are. Our emotional perception is different from the reality in which we operate. We think that we are ugly, boring, stupid, or some other awful thing, when in reality, we are loved, admired, and encouraged by others.

When we start to place these judgements and restrictions on ourselves, then we are holding our future back and lacking progression. We have to see and accept our worth so that we can better become the people that we are truly meant to be.

How This Strategy Changes Your Perspective

To separate oneself from their emotional reactions in order to control judgement is one of the simplest tips for stoics, but also one of the most challenging to start. We have conditioned ourselves to feel emotions and act directly from what they invoke.

Some people that are only based in emotion are seen as passionate, and that can be admirable.

This can be true sometimes, but a stoic will strive to not be driven by passion, which we'll get to later in the book.

When you start to question your emotions, they will be much easier to regulate. Remember that feelings are not facts, so when you start to think a certain way, and that thought becomes something that will help you make a decision, then remember to fully investigate before acting.

It's not always easy to admit that we are acting on emotion either. There are some situations where we'd rather not admit that we are reacting emotionally. This will be challenging, but we have to continually confront our inner thoughts so that we can become virtuous.

We also often start to realize that what we feel is usually caused by something else, a deeper issue. If one small thing angers you, then there's likely a bigger issue that inflates the situation. If everyone thinks something is fine but it is upsetting you, then ask yourself what happened to change your perspective and make it different from others.

This will help you discover a deeper truth that could grow your virtue.

It's hard in the beginning, but it becomes a lot easier as time goes on.

Eventually, you will find that you are indifferent to a lot of things, making it easier for you to make better judgments and live more contently.

Indifference is something that is achieved, and that is a good virtue to have. It doesn't mean that you don't have strong morals, or that you are weaker in any way.

It simply means that you can take in all realities and make correct judgements.

What it's Like Before you Recognized This

Before you realize only you are in control of your emotions, you will feel helpless by different instances, trapped in various circumstances. You might feel like there is no way out, and nothing ever satisfies you. Perhaps you even struggle with addiction of some sort to help you through situations that are more challenging. When you realize you are in control of your judgements, it can be freeing.

We can tunnel ourselves into a place where we create strict rules that govern our judgments. What happens is that we become harsh of how we see others. We can look at the things a person has done and determine if they are good or bad based on the decisions they've made. It can be easy to overlook a person for who they really are rather than what we've concluded based on the little information we know.

Then, we start to cast judgments on ourselves. The harsher we are on others, the harsher we are on ourselves. When we let go of judgement, it makes the world a lot easier to be a part of.

Rather than going around and becoming upset that certain things don't go how we thought they would, separating ourselves from emotion means that we make better judgements.

How Things are Better Now as a Result of Practicing

When emotions are more easily regulated, it becomes a lot simpler to process the hard ones as they come. When emotions are out of control, then it can seem like everything else in life is as well. If a person becomes easily angry, anxious, upset, scared, or are generally sensitive to feeling certain emotions, then it will start to drive how they interact in the world. If they are often scared of their surroundings, then they will certainly avoid various situations.

When we remember that our emotions do not define who we are, that opens up so many doors. When you lose the fear, shame, anger, or any other heavy emotion that holds you back, then you will start to feel like more things are accomplished than you ever could have imagined.

Some might think stoics won't feel as excited, then, when they are not acting on emotion.

It's quite the opposite, however. Stoics will feel these positive emotions more. Because they have learned how to endure the pain and make the most of it, they will know exactly how they can take the most from the positive emotion as well.

This means appreciating everything that it brings, being mindful throughout the experience, and remembering how it felt so that those positive emotions can carry them through the darker times later on.

When I Started Practicing This

During the darker times when I was unhappy with my life, I would often fantasize about different things I looked forward to happening. I would be stressed about paying a bill, so I would lay in bed and imagine a life where I had money as I fell asleep. The bills kept coming, but I would keep dreaming of a better life.

What I didn't realize was, however, that I was setting myself up for disappointment. I started to create a world that I was happy in. Eventually, this world became the only way I believed I could ever be happy.

It felt impossible to feel good if I wasn't imagining this better life. I was so miserable with what was going on around me that I had escaped into a different world, and that wasn't productive.

It was an unhealthy and endless cycle that I wouldn't be able to break as long as I didn't see it was happening.

I would also judge other people, and some things others did offend me. It was easy to see every action another person did as an attack against me. This was because I was validating that I was an unhappy, unlikable person. I was looking for realistic ways to devalue my life in order to help emphasize that this fantasy I created was the real world, making me feel like it was eventually going to come to me.

After years of escaping to a different, better life, I realized that I wasn't ever going to get there if I didn't focus on what was happening right now. Stoicism helped me to realize that no matter how terrible my situation seemed, I still had the power it took to be happy. Only then could I have the time and emotional energy to do what needed to be done.

I was feeling my emotions too hard! These chemical reactions that I barely understood were the captain of my life. A stoic understands that they must use logic in order to help them decide what is the right thing to do in life.

Living in Maintained Control

As I've controlled my emotions, I've been able to better rationalize my actions, therefore, much of what I feel is easier to manage.

Emotions will always be there, and it's up to me to remember that I always have control. Some days are harder than others, but I don't have those, "worst day" feelings anymore. No matter how much I want to emotionally react in any given scenario, I always remind myself that things aren't as bad as they seem, and patience will always be the best solution.

It's also important for me to remember that I need to feel even the bad emotions, as they will make me stronger. They are just as powerful as the good things I feel. I used to try and avoid anything bad, but then I remembered that even these negative emotions don't have to be labeled as bad anymore. They are harder to feel, and I prefer to feel them less, but they are still good in that they help me define my virtue.

Chapter 8

Nature has Always Been and Will Always Be Outside of Your Control

The operations of the universe are beyond our knowledge. As much as humans like to try and guess what will happen, make predictions, and hope for a better future, we will never really know what lies ahead. There are certain predictions that we can make, and we can cross out other outcomes from happening, but the answer will only ever be revealed as we are living through the experiences we have predicted.

Nature must be faced and accepted as a process. It is not one instance, a simple truth, or an easy explanation. Nature is something that happens, for lack of better terms, naturally. This means without resistance, in accordance with what is expected, and accepting of reality. This does not mean that we should no longer be resistant. If we are to live in a way that is expected, then how would anything ever change?

That is a common issue that people run into when mentioning "in accordance with nature." What we have to remember, however, is that if everyone were already living in accordance with nature, then there wouldn't be any issues that we have to fix. The world wouldn't be perfect, but it would work itself out.

The resistance of nature, people acting in ways that are in line with greed, temptation, and overall lack of virtue is what is causing issues, and if this stopped, then other parts of nature would fall into place.

Do not allow natural process to invade peace of mind. Part of living in accordance with nature is the acceptance that not everything will be perfect either. Since there are so many people in the world, there will always be opposing views. There might not always be war, but there will always be conflict.

We have to be accepting of this. We don't have to allow it to happen with all of its consequence, but we do have to be aware that trying to avoid anything negative is not in accordance with nature. A stoic understands the balance between good and bad.

Do not be disturbed by external circumstances. Those events that you cannot change shouldn't be things that lead your emotions and how you react. You have to learn how to be accepting of the things that come to us that we have little power over. You won't have control over what your external circumstances are, but you will be able to take charge of the way that you react to these things.

It's important to understand the difference between influence and control as well. When you influence something, it's like guiding a floating boat in water.

You might make waves and help push it in a certain direction, but where the boat goes will ultimately be determined by other factors.

Control is when you are in the boat, steering the wheel. There are many things that we have control over, and more that we can influence. Learn the difference and you will discover that you are able to put emphasis on more important things in your life.

We also have to understand the translations of stoic writings, in that nature is often taken from "phusis," which doesn't mean what we always think of as nature, such as primates, animalistic behavior, the outdoors, and all things green.

When we are saying "live in accordance with nature," that doesn't mean you have to ditch your house and live off the land. It's not talking about nature in a way we commonly interpret, such as trees, animals, plants, wind, water, air, and other natural elements. When stoics were discussing living in accordance with nature, they were talking about living a life with phusis.

Phusis could also refer to evolution, or the attempt at nature refining itself, ridding of the excess, and forming more perfect versions throughout time. When we are living in accordance with nature, this is what we should be doing. Define yourself based on your circumstance.

This definition isn't a set of rules that you have to live by, rather, the unique qualities that help to determine who you are as an individual.

Living in accordance with nature means using only what is needed and ridding ourselves of what we might include as unnecessary fluff.

Stoics thought that phusis was the way that we should live, or the flow that needs accepting. It's not about "being perfect," or even "seeking perfection." It's understanding that perfect, or whatever similar word you might use to describe an ideally happy life, isn't a point in time that you will reach, but rather, the process of accepting that you should always seek growth.

An Olympic athlete isn't perfect because they got perfect scores in their event. A "perfect" Olympic athlete is one that continues to improve their talents, showing consistent growth and success within their achieved field. There is no avoiding nature and trying to change it to better ourselves. Instead, we have to live with nature and be our best in the circumstances that we are presented with, no matter how much influence or control we might have (Aurelius, 2019).

Our level of Influence on Nature

How we live in accordance with nature is important to understand because it will help us to define our virtues. If you are consistently trying to push your ideas onto others, force things to go your way, or living in an individual world rather than seeing your role as a whole, then one would argue this is out of nature's path.

Though it might feel virtuous, you must ask if it is something that is really helping the natural flow of things. By checking your influence on nature and how you are using that, then you will be able to better judge whether your actions are virtuous.

Some individuals would like to think they have complete control over their lives, others would think that they have none. A stoic understands that they have both. A stoic won't try to gain more power either. They will take influence as it comes if others are willing to be influenced by them, but they will not seek out places of power. They will also not hide their opinion should they feel as though it needs to be heard, but a stoic is very good at understanding whether what they have to share will actually be useful to others.

A stoic knows that there is a varying degree of influence we have on nature. You can go hunting and choose to shoot a deer, eat it, and repeat the process, getting better at hunting, and cooking, growing those skills.

You can also go out and study the deer, better understanding how they operate, what they eat, and what their behavior is like. You can grow your knowledge of these animals. Whether or not these acts are in accordance with nature is going to be up to you to determine, but if you felt that they are so, then you could determine based on your ideas that this is an act of virtue as well, as you are seeking prudence.

Whether you believe nature is controlled by an outside source such as gods or goddesses is irrelevant. What is true is that parts of nature will always be uncontrollable. While you might have the power to shoot a deer, you still won't be able to control whether or not that deer has a disease that will make you sick, or if one year, deer go extinct from over-hunting, or if deer start attacking hunters as well. All of these things are unlikely, but they would be out of our control if they happened. Reflecting on instances like these is important so we can understand our level of influence on nature.

High Influence

We have a high influence over our choices in judgments and actions. While nature is out of our control, our judgements are completely in our control. It doesn't always feel this way. Sometimes you might make a judgement based on what you think you should believe. Perhaps a religious leader, teacher, or other role model held a certain belief, and you used that to make some judgements. While they might have seemed in control over our decisions, they only influenced how we felt. We were the ones that ultimately decided the way to believe.

What your opinion is happens to be based on many things, but it is still completely up to you. When someone says, "that's just my opinion," feel free to remind them that you can change it! Your opinion will be unique to you and it will feel natural, but we always have total control over what we will decide to think.

What you want to pursue is entirely up to you. If you want to move to a different country, or go back to school to change careers, that is all completely in your power.

Only you can decide whether or not this is something that you want to do. Some people might try to control these actions, but you are always in control at the end of the day.

Whether or not that challenge will be easy is not in your control, but the desire is the property of no one but you. Your actions are also up to you. It can often feel as though you are not in control of your actions, and someone else might have made you so angry or annoyed that you did something you regret.

Regardless of how much influence they might have had over your emotions, you were still the person that was in control of this feeling.

These things can all be heavily influenced to the point where we feel like we might not have control over them. However, it's important that we recognize when we do so that we can do our best to take control.

These are all the things that we have high influence over.

Partial Influence

Our health, wealth, relationships, and the outcomes of our behaviors are all things that we have a partial influence over.

You can choose to exercise daily and eat only healthy foods, but there is always the risk of a rare disease, cancer, or some other health ailment that can't be prevented through lifestyle choices.

You can influence your health, but you can't completely control it. Age is part of our health as well. Many individuals will live lives where they try and avoid age, going through dangerous procedures or uncomfortable measures to make themselves feel younger.

We will have some influence over how the effects of aging will alter our health, but we don't have influence over whether or not we will age.

We can try to influence our status and wealth, but there will always be restrictions we have to work within. If you were born into poverty, you can try and change how much money you make, but you will have much lower chances of attaining a high status as opposed to someone born into it.

The relationships we share belong to someone else as well, so we can't always assume control over them. You can choose to be a loving spouse, always going out of your way to show affection and maintaining faithfulness, but you won't be able to control if your partner does the same.

You can influence them to be better, and how you act will likely reflect on them in certain ways, but some people will just be unable to grow with you.

No Influence

We have almost no influence on the weather, our ethnicity, and most external circumstances. You can't decide if someone else is going to cause a disaster, or if a different country decides to rage war against your native lands if you're not in a place of political power.

Until we prove the science of what our existence is, if at all, before we were born into this earth, we can't say that we chose to be born to the parents we had. We have no influence on our blood relatives,

and very little influence on the people we are geographically close to up until a certain age.

War is another thing we can't control. You might be able to influence it, but most of us have absolutely no control in whether or not a war is occurring in our country. If you are the president, you have way more control, but as a citizen on an individual level, even as an active voter you have almost no influence over wars occurring in our world.

Recycling and taking care of the environment can help to reduce damage to the earth as a whole, but we won't be able to personally affect hurricanes, rainfall, sweltering hot days, and how much pollen is in the air. You also won't be able to influence whether or not you have these allergies. Understanding that these things are out of our control is important if we want to move forward in a healthy way.

The Flow of Events is Beyond Your Control

We have to learn how to accept what is. At the same time, we can't let ourselves be totally powerless. There should be an emphasis on always determining what is and is not in our control. From there, we can learn to accept what is not, and change things as we can.

It's not about trying to make predictions about what will happen. It's about looking back on what has happened and understanding that it all served a purpose. It can be a hard idea to grasp when we start discussing all of the things that are out of our control.

Thinking of a war in another country that we can't change can be hard to handle. The emphasis shouldn't be looking at this event and wishing it wasn't happening, or desperately hoping for ways that we can change it. What we should do instead is find ways to accept it for what it is.

Sometimes, thinks that aren't related to nature are still just "natural" in the sense that they are an expected part of life – death by car accidents, declaring bankruptcy, developing heart disease – these things are unfortunate, certainly aren't a naturally occurring event in the sense of nature, but they are things that happen in life.

While you might have had initial control over how things have flowed, there's no going back now.

The person that ate fast food every day didn't intentionally gain weight, but they did, and now they have to move forward and work with that situation. There's no going back or preventing it now. Back to the analogy of water, when you send a wave, it has a ripple effect.

You can choose to send the wave, but once you have, you can't stop the ripples from spreading throughout the rest of the water. This is important to remember as we are defining the line between the things we can and can't control. While it might seem like you can control the future, you have to ask yourself if you also have to deal with the rest of the ripples that you had initially sent.

Something like bankruptcy doesn't seem natural at all, but it might be a part of nature you live in accordance with. If after years of struggling with debt and no way seemingly out of it, bankruptcy might be something that you have to come face to face with and accept, no matter how challenging or frustrating that thought might be.

The things that seem like they are avoidable might be what we have to accept, and the things that seem out of our control might also be the things we need to realize we can change.

How to Deal with Natural Processes Effectively

Aside from what we talked about in the last section, there are a lot of natural processes that we can't stop.

Aging is the biggest one.

You must first deal with these issues by facing them. Avoiding them is never going to do you any good and will in fact cause harm. The longer you push something off, the harder it is going to be to deal with once you get there.

We can assume, in reference to the first section of this chapter, that nature, in a stoic sense, is what is expected from reality, and what is certain. With that being said, we also have to remember that uncertainty itself is one of the few things that we will always have to depend on.

While you can prevent losing your house financially, you won't always be able to prevent a fire. You can make sure to never leave any candles lit, but you can't control if your apartment neighbors are going to do the same.

To deal with these processes, we mustn't force ourselves to think within the constraints of what "natural" should be, because this, itself, is unnatural.

Desires and Emotions are a Part of Nature

We have natural urges. You will always feel hunger, which will lead to you eating, which will lead to the certain feeling that you will have to go to the bathroom.

Beyond these simple things, we have larger desires. We will always want to have others around us. We will want to have some form of possession, whether it's a home, money, or niche collection.

When we accept that this is natural and don't try to change how we feel, it will in turn be easier to change how we react to that emotion.

Don't try to avoid anything. Take it all in as it should be. Don't deny your urge to be around others but be mindful of the way that this desire might make you act. Don't make yourself feel bad for wanting material things, but understand what deeper desires are present that make you want to seek out these possessions.

Use everything as a resource, even the challenging things. No desire or emotion you feel should be something that you deny, or something that you let drive you. As all stoics would do, find the balance. Accept the emotion for what it is and explore why it is something that can seemingly have so much power over you.

How This Strategy Changes Your Perception

When you realize that you should essentially, "go with the flow," life can really open up with you. We don't think Seneca would ever say something as simple, but it's an easy way for us to process the idea now. This mentality helps you to find a balance between preparing for the future while still expecting surprises.

When you can better determine what you have influence over and what you should just let be, you can feel more in control of your life.

It can be easy to try and plan everything as well. While it's good to create structure, planning things can actually derail you. You will realize you can start to get things done, because you plan realistically.

What it's Like Before you Recognized This

Before you recognize the restrictions of your natural control, it can seem like life is a mess. You might have certain expectations that are never met, and life can feel disappointing when your visions are never fulfilled.

We sometimes reach for control in other ways when attempting to feel like we have power in our life. Humans can do some strange things when they are on the path for power, and when they look for it in ways that they can't control, then it can make them act irrationally.

In an attempt to gain control, we often wind up feeling powerless. Once you start to find the things you have control over, you will feel more powerful knowing that even though you aren't entirely in charge, you are still influential.

How Things are Better Now as a Result of Practicing

The only true freedom you have in this life is whether or not something is going to make you feel a certain way.

You can choose whether you're going to eat a burger or a taco for dinner, but you don't get to choose whether or not you're still hungry.

It is a freeing feeling when we start to let go of the things that we can't change. It's not like we should ignore these parts of life, but it will make them seem less scary when we learn how to accept them.

When I Started Practicing This

I, like many individuals in this massive world, have worked multiple different jobs throughout my life. Some I worked nights cleaning tables, others I sat behind a desk typing all day. Whatever the job, they all had one thing in common – I disliked them.

I was living my life weekend to weekend, only happy on my days off. It was challenging going to work every day, knowing that I was going to have to confront the same meaningless activity that put me in a bad mood the night before. I was waiting for a point in my life where I would be happy, not realizing how much time I was wasting being miserable.

I also realized that I was waiting around for something else to happen. I was expecting myself to be able to change things I had no control over, while waiting for something else to happen with the things that were in the realm of my abilities.

Living in Maintained Control

By recognizing I'm not entirely in control has still given me back power because I can focus on what matters the most.

When I accept that I can't plan everything in my life, while also understanding that my destiny is in my control, it helps me better decide what needs my attention.

All of the things that I was trying to achieve, desperately going against nature, these were just my preferred indifference. What matters most is that I am virtuous, and this is done as I navigate through life, not one particular time.

There is no endpoint. I am not living life so that I can reach one point of happiness and that be it. Life isn't about saving money and then spending it on one thing. It's not about going crazy and spending it all the time either.

Take each day as it is but keep tomorrow in mind.

Chapter 9

Do Not Be Consumed by Your Passions

This next tip helps transition from the last, as we have to make sure we are doing another important thing - live in accordance with nature. Passion is a strong and barely controllable emotion. Even when we think we have it figured out, there can still be underlying drivers that we aren't fully aware of. It is necessary as a tool for advancement but a destructive driver. Emotion isn't based in logic, disregarding of the past warnings and future problems.

Some have carried the misconception that stoics often deny the existence of emotion. It's not that they are in denial, it's just that certain emotions of ours must not be emphasized. Rather than allowing anger to be a driving force in a stoic's decision, they would sit through those feelings of discomfort and handle the situation appropriately.

Passios, in Latin, also known as pathos, is different than what we understand to be emotion in English. The translations are where things get tricky when unpacking the common ideas of stoics. When we think of passion, it can go a few ways. someone might be passionate when they are speaking, but you might also consider having an interest in music a passion (Graver, 2007).

When analyzing stoic material, most passion translations are in reference to strong emotional drivers.

A stoic doesn't think that it is wrong to have a passion, but it would not be in accordance with nature to let certain passionate emotions we feel derail our plans.

Your passion is when you can't control your emotional cravings that are driven by desire. Jealous rage can cause a passionate person to spy on their lover if they feel they are being unfaithful. Wanting to win

a competition can cause someone to act on their passions and hurt their competitors to help them get ahead. A stoic would not act in such ways and would approach the situation logically. It is not that they wouldn't feel those initial emotions first, but they would know how to work through them so that they don't cause destructive behavior.

You don't want to be void of all passion. It's simply that we cannot let them control our thoughts. When you do, then you can fall into negative thinking patterns. When you feel a passionate thought coming into your head, maybe something along the lines of, "I hate her," "this is awful," "nothing is going right," recognize that these are passionate statements.

You're not just making a comment about one thing, rather, an assumption of many ideas as a whole. Question these thoughts and figure out what the emotions are that are causing you to feel these passionate beliefs.

Do you hate her because you are jealous? Is this just awful because you are tired? Does nothing feel like it's going right because multiple negative things occurred in a row? When you can look inwards and see what is driving your passionate thoughts, it will be easier to see that you are allowing emotion to have too much power.

We believe happiness comes from being passionate about something and fulfilling those passions.

What we need to realize is that this won't bring us a virtuous life. Having that initial passion, seeing where it came from and where it can go is going to be the happy part. Allowing our passions to grow and using them in a positive way can be virtuous.

As long as we are focused on looking inward and seeing what the real desire is, we can determine how it will benefit our virtue. Only then can you control your passions to work for you rather than allowing them to consume you.

The True Understanding of Things

There are certain kinds of passions that we must understand. These will be the things you are naturally passionate about, your friends and family. You might be passionate about a hobby, like painting or cooking.

We are passionate about our pets, our children, our neighbors, the environment, comedy, food, and all other great things that bring happiness in life.

These are good passions as long as we are still living in accordance with nature along with them.

We have different pre-passions that we should be aware of. These are natural emotional reactions to certain stimuli.

You might experience anxiety or fear over something coming soon. This is a passion that you cannot let consume you. Unhealthy passion would include suffering through something, realizing you made a bad decision, or rather, the feeling that you did so.

Fear in general can be dangerous because it is usually irrational. Being envious and jealous can be unhealthy passions because you aren't fully understanding of the situation. When we are jealous, we exhibit some sort of lust or desire, but only for the good things, ignoring the bad or other challenges that might have come along.

These are our emotional reactions. The better you can understand if your emotional reaction is a healthy or unhealthy passion, the easier it will be to see the truth of the situation and work towards a better solution, or some other form of improvement.

You are not driven by your emotions. You are driven by the true understanding of things.

You Live by Specific Principles

"If you live in harmony with nature you will never be poor; if you live according to what others think, you will never be rich." — Seneca, Letters from a Stoic (Seneca, 65 AD)

We fall into a place where we believe that we cannot be happy without our passions. This is where stoics will develop the biggest issues.

It is important to live by specific principles, that stoicism can help form, so that you do not allow passion to consume you. When you are having trouble deciding whether passion is controlling you, the stoic principles we have been discussing so far are what is going to drive you.

You do Not Give Into Temptations

When you can control your passion, you will not give into temptations. We don't always recognize that something was a temptation until after we've already decided to indulge. Do not reprimand yourself should you fall into temptation every once in a while but recognize when this has happened. Use the experience as one to learn and grow from. The only one we are hurting when giving into temptation is ourselves.

We often think of passionate people as those that care more than others.

Perhaps they are simply more reckless, and willing to show that they are driven by natural instinct rather than collected reflection.

Stoics will aim to define the line between what is natural passion, what urges we feel, and the passion that we grow within ourselves, choosing what we want to put an emphasis on the most.

Passion Can be the Enemy of Control if it's Not Contained

If we consistently question our value judgements and are always trying to alter our virtues, then it will be much easier to ensure that we are not being too driven by a false passion. Positive passion is that which gives you beneficial emotions. Start to focus more on things that bring positive passion rather than those that elicit more feelings of negative passion. Don't mistake the two and be honest with yourself when self-reflecting.

There is only one thing that will always seem to be truly beneficial, and that is virtue. As long as you are growing, learning, and doing your best to become someone more virtuous than yesterday, then you will be living in accordance with nature and you will find happiness comes easier and more frequently.

Many individuals think that money will give them happiness and spend their life chasing this passion.

It is not a true virtue because with it you can be unhappy, and many other individuals are able to be happy without it. When you are continually building your virtues, this is when you will be more at peace with yourself.

A stoic will live their life not denying passion but ensuring that their value judgements aren't wrong. They allow passion into their lives, but only as something that exists, not a direct ruler.

How This Strategy Changes Your Perception

When first exposed to stoicism, I thought perhaps it meant being emotionless.

I would consistently read about passion and how it shouldn't be a driver in the way that we act or play any indication in our behavior.

As a previously passionate person, it seemed as though this would be challenging, but made sense if I wanted to change my perspective and life for the better, in general.

What I eventually realized, however, was that stoicism isn't about having no emotion.

Instead, it's controlling them better.

This means that you aren't ignoring good feelings, but you're emphasizing them even more, and giving that energy that you used to have for your negative emotions to those.

This changes your perception because you can better understand what is actually important in your life rather than what you just felt negatively passionate about.

What it's Like Before you Recognized This

We are passionate about things that we wouldn't fully care about if someone else hadn't put that idea there in the first place.

Many people might find that they are passionate about their job, but only because they are afraid of being poor. Others might think that being passionate about material things is what drives them, but really, they just like the security of these objects as it alleviates their negative passions.

How Things are Better Now as a Result of Practicing

When you start to differentiate the passions and take control over them once again rather than letting them play the role of leader, then it becomes much easier to know what you need to focus on in this life.

Rather than giving into passion that is meaningless, you can take the precious time we have and put it towards beneficial passion that not only brings you happiness but helps others as well.

When I Started Practicing This

I started practicing this after I realized that I was living a life that wasn't my own. I was working a job I disliked so that I could buy expensive things that didn't even bring me that much joy. I was dating someone that I thought I was passionate about, but in reality, I simply liked the security the idea of them brought. I was unhappy, and one day I realized I didn't want to be anymore.

The more I studied stoicism, the more I realized that I can better evaluate the emotions that I'm feeling. Rather than acting on urges and going with my gut all the time, I am taking a minute to self- reflect. I can still "go with my gut," but that's because it's more controlled now, and I have the tools I need to dig deeper into my passions.

Living in Maintained Control

Living in maintained control becomes easier as a result of practicing not letting my passions consume me.

I can more easily look at my life objectively and ask if I am doing something because I want to, because it is a beneficial act for my virtue, or if I am simply acting on negative passion that I have allowed to consume me.

Chapter 10

Always Avoid Being Excessive or Deficient

You do not need to have, do, or be more than is necessary, normal, or desirable. There is always an underlying reason that some individuals will have for wanting more than is necessary. A person that is greedy with money, someone that is gluttonous with food, or an individual that takes advantage of time usually has something driving that desire, most commonly a negative passion. We are all excessive every once in a while, but at the same time, you can't live a life surrounded by this.

In contrast, for no reason, require yourself to not have enough of a specified quality or ingredient in order to maintain your natural standards. Not being excessive doesn't mean that we should be deficient either. It is important to be generous, giving, and sometimes sacrificial. We also are deserving of things ourselves, and we should require them in our lives still. The things we should be excessive with are our virtues. We cannot place an emphasis on pleasing other people or living up to their standards. This reason, along with the desire for pleasurable experiences, often drives us to be excessive.

"Never depend on the admiration of others. There is no strength in it. Personal merit cannot be derived from an external source.

It is not to be found in your personal associations, nor can it be found in the regard of other people.

It is a fact of life that other people, even people who love you, will not necessarily agree with your ideas, understand you, or share your enthusiasms. Grow up! Who cares what other people think about you!" – Epictetus (Epictetus, 1595)

It's important to understand the balance of our virtues. We need to have high standards when it comes to questioning them and defining them. Similarly, we cannot be too strict with them either. There should be no limit on how many virtuous experiences we go through, but we cannot force some things to happen if it is not in accordance with nature.

When you are too far on one end of the spectrum, then you will end up taking something to the extreme level, having more consequence than what was there before the extreme virtue was met. Even though something that we are seeking might be in line with one of our virtues, that does not mean that seeking it in excess is still virtuous.

You can be too ambitious. You will either end up being insatiable or blinded with false purpose. On the other hand, no ambition can lead to having little to no desire. A stoic knows how to find the balance in between these two ends of the spectrum of excess and deficiency.

Empathy is another important virtue.

Too much can mean that you are dependent on other people, and you might start to overlook your own feelings.

Not enough means that you will struggle to have proper emotion for others, leading to narcissistic tendencies.

Other virtues include adaptability, confidence levels, discipline, and state of nature. Though it might seem good to have more of a certain virtue, it can still be excessive. We have to continue to live in accordance with nature and always find the right balance between "too much," and "not enough."

Accepting Nature

We don't just need to accept ourselves for the face value of human nature. It's important to understand nature as a whole, and how it interacts with others. There are humans, animals, plants, weather elements, and things far beyond the sky that we don't have control over.

We might be able to guess how things ended up the way they are, and others will use religion to fill the gaps for what existence, and nature, is. All of that doesn't matter to stoics. Instead, the focus is on accepting nature for what it is.

We cannot change it and knowing why it is here won't necessarily make it any different than it is now.

We have to do what we can to accept it.

It's not about trying to change things to be better or changing our perspective so that things seem better.

It's about learning how to handle even the most challenging situations, because even pain can be productive, no matter how much we might try and avoid it. Accepting nature is going to help you to find the balance between excess and deficiency.

Nonresistance

Don't wish for reality to be any different than it is. Be happy for what it is now, even if it seems bad. There are things that can be worse, and things that can be better. Imagining these scenarios won't change anything. We must be non resistant to the truth, to reality.

If you are too rigid, it becomes harder to accept nature for what it is. Be open to new ideas and accept that you are still going to have times of struggle in the future. That is nothing to fear. Instead, it's a reminder that we should always work to strengthen our beliefs to be prepared.

At the same time, we cannot become too open of the future or else we risk becoming soft. If you try and remove your virtue, have no morals, and take everything in as good because it is easier, then this won't bring happiness. It is a lack of virtue, which can lead to a feeling of lack of purpose.

Non Judgment

Don't judge events, simply accept them as they are. You will still have judgements slip in naturally, because our brains have been conditioned to be judgmental. Remember to always look at the opposing side, and allow yourself to see all judgements, never fully believing in one singular one.

Our judgements are among the things that we have the most control over. This is why we should be focusing on not allowing them to have control over us.

Our judgements do not need to be punished – we simply should use them as a tool to self-reflect. Where did these judgements form? Even if we don't like to admit we had a certain judgement, it's still important to reflect on it to determine how we can prevent it from having weight in our mind in the future.

Non Attachment

Things come and go, don't get too attached to what you like. It's important to be passionate about good things, but also accept that they are fleeting. Just because one good thing is ending doesn't mean that you will never experience good again. We cannot stay too attached because then we will get too comfortable.

A stoic knows they should always strive for comfortability.

"There is no enjoying the possession of anything valuable unless one has someone to share it with" – Lucius Annaeus Seneca (Seneca, 65 AD)

Sharing things is an important part of stoic philosophy. This can help bring you to new levels of joy you weren't expecting in the first place.

How This Strategy Changes Your Perception

When you stay humble, you are showing that the only thing you need is your virtue. This will help you achieve the happiness that all stoics are seeking. Rather than placing weight on material things, objects of desire, and activities that give immense pleasure, you will no longer be excessive. This helps you to appreciate what you have

now much better. You will also realize that sharing the things you love helps to keep you from being deficient as well.

What it's Like Before you Recognized This

Before this happens, it's much easier to be consumed by your passions. It's easier to see how the many principles we've been discussing connect with each other so well.

When you can articulate one virtue and express that in a positive way, it becomes much easier to do so for all the others.

How Things are Better Now as a Result of Practicing

Things are better now as a result of practicing because it is much easier to be happy. Rather than constantly needing new stimuli and more things to bring pleasure, a stoic can find that they are satisfied with all the beauty that they were overlooking before.

When I Started Practicing This

I started practicing this because I was way too obsessed with material things. I would look at wealthy celebrities and feel jealous I didn't have what they did. I would spend all my money on things I thought would make me happy, like clothes, food, furniture, and vacations. These were all moments of luxury instead of things that were actually bringing me any joy. I realized as I practiced stoicism, that I was completely fine without my stuff, much happier in fact.

Living in Maintained Control

I have been able to live in maintained control after giving up excess and deficiency. It is much easier to focus on the important things that actually bring me joy. I still shop for clothes, but instead of buying designer labels to impress others, I get durable, practical clothes. I buy things that fit in with a style that makes me feel unique, not something that I think will help me fit in with others.

I still eat good food, but instead of eating huge portions, I look for ways to be creative with healthy cooking. I still go on vacations as well. Instead of finding the most luxurious hotel, I seek out new adventure in places that aren't vacationed often in order to help broaden my experiences.

There is a way to still have the happy things in life without being excessive. It's all about living in accordance with nature and questioning your passions.

Chapter 11

You Deserve and Require Evidence, Reason, or Proof

As a stoic, you should understand that it's important we accept situations for what they are, and we don't try to go too outside of our realm to change what we cannot control. This is the balance that all stoics will try to achieve on their journey of virtue.

That being said, it's also important that stoics aren't just living an "it is what it is" lifestyle. While we have to learn to accept things, and patience and understanding are a huge part of stoicism, we still deserve real knowledge surrounding the things that we choose to believe.

Stoics will always look for evidence, reason, or proof before making a judgement. We are keeping this last because it is applicable to all of the other stoic principles that we have discussed so far. A common theme throughout this book has been the acceptance of certain things that are out of our control. This should never be confused with accepting false information, or not digging further into a questionable subject simply because we cannot change it.

Stoics understand that it's important to take more information in so that we can be assured we are understanding of reality, not just a perception created only on the face value of minor investigations.

When a fact is heard, it should be solidified with evidence. When someone is making a claim, they need to have good reason behind it. When we are confronted with information we don't immediately believe, we deserve proof (Pigliucci, 2019).

Taking Things into Consideration

There are certain things you have to investigate before taking anything into consideration. First, always look at the source of the information.

Sometimes this is a close friend, or maybe it's a trusted news site. Though this is your source for the version they're giving you, it's not always going to be the actual information that is true.

While this is something we have to consider, it's also important to remember that we shouldn't accuse, or call people out, just because they don't have all of the facts right away. As a stoic yourself, you shouldn't make claims until you are entirely knowledgeable about the fact. However, when others do this, you should not condemn them, as they are already hurting themselves by making these assumptions in their own mind.

Facts

We require a solid body of facts or information indicating whether a belief or proposition is true or valid before taking certain things into consideration.

Just because a belief is something that is passionately held, that doesn't make it true. We always need to look at the solid facts behind a situation. This also means the real truth of something, not the way that it was spun. This is seen often with many news articles online today. They will sensationalize a story and use clickbait to make a small fact seem like something huge. A stoic knows that just because something seems like it is true, that doesn't mean it is entirely factual.

Considering facts is going to be important when determining whether or not you should give into your emotions or passions. Someone might have hurt you.

Is it a fact that they were trying to hurt you? Just because we might have strongly felt that they were intentionally hurting us doesn't mean that they actually meant to.

Facts, logical evidence that cannot be disputed, is important to make assured judgements.

When something can be discussed, that doesn't mean it is a lie, but if it can be disputed with other factual claims, then it is not, after all, a fact.

Cause, Explanation, or Justification

We have to consider a worthy cause, explanation, or justification for an action or event. Nothing happens just because. There is always going to be a reason behind it happening, no matter how small it might be.

A stoic isn't going to agonize over looking for a cause, but they are not going to let a virtue, or any belief, be true to them, unless they can find the cause, explanation, and justification behind something.

Cause can help us to determine what things we might need to improve on in the future. If you can recognize the cause of your mood or behavior, then you're going to be able to prevent against any destruction it could cause in the future.

Explanation is going to be helpful when we are confronted with things that we do not understand. Explanation is also necessary when we are developing quick judgements based on minimal information that we are given. This is often seen in "scientific" articles.

Justification helps us to understand and accept the reason that something might have occurred. Though we might not have always known why it happened in the first place, we can at least find a reason that it is important after the fact.

Verification of the Truth

Facts are going to be necessary to verify the truth behind a statement. It isn't always easy to verify everything, but a stoic will still seek out the authenticity behind the things that they choose to believe.

Just because we believe something to be true at once doesn't mean that it will always remain true. As stoics get older, they understand that they need to consistently go back and find the verification of a truth, even if it's something that they've believed in for a long time.

It's important that we have virtue but not to the point that it blinds us into thinking there is only one truth.

Someone truly virtuous understands that all experiences make us different, therefore we are always going to have differing viewpoints on certain virtues.

When we think that something is true, we should still question to determine if our perspectives have been altered. Not everything is going to have numerical evidence and scientific tests to back it up, but that doesn't mean we can't still believe it to be true. What's important is ensuring that we never fully allow ourselves to believe something is true unless we have logical reasoning behind why it cannot be false.

What will Start to Happen as a result of Practicing this Strategy

When you start to require evidence, reason, and proof behind everything that you take in, you will start to realize that nothing is ever as it seems.

We too often take things in at face value, but when you start to always say, "is that really true?" you will realize that most things aren't as factual as they will try to claim to be in the beginning.

What it's Like Before you Recognized This

Before recognizing this, it can start to feel like everything is intense, and most things you encounter will seem different. Reading a news story headline can make it seem like the world is ending and listening to stories from others will make you question yourself far too often.

How Things are Better Now as a Result of Practicing

Once you start to question everything, you will open up so many doors you never would have walked through in the first place. You can realize many things you used to believe aren't nearly as true as you thought. You will also learn a lot more in the process. On the pursuit of truth, you end up finding many more questions that you will also need to find a factual answer to.

When I Started Practicing This

I started practicing this after I found myself addicted to online news stories. I would wake up anxious to open my phone and see the new scary titles about how my favorite drink caused cancer, or there was a high chance of getting attacked in my area. After a while, I realized that I was actually seeking out these more anxiety-inducing news stories.

I started to investigate the truth of these articles after I discovered that I was letting them dictate my actions, beliefs, and mood. The deeper I dug, the more I realized that a lot of the articles I was reading would lead back to the same source.

Though five different articles were giving me different information, they all had the same source, and simply twisted that to suit their "brand," "aesthetic," or whatever else they needed to in order to get people like me to click.

The more I investigated these topics, the more I was able to diffuse the hype surrounding them. On my pursuit of the truth, I found more reliable sources as well, and am able to better draw my own conclusions rather than desperately clinging to the words of others that are trying to simply freak me out.

Living in Maintained Control

I have been able to live in maintained control better, because I am always questioning the validity of the information I get. Rather than getting worried because I hear something frightening, I wait a moment and look at the reality of the situation.

This doesn't just go for news articles, but for gossip as well. Rather than buying into the things that other people would tell me, I instead focus on reality and making my own investigations and conclusions to find the truth.

Chapter 12

Putting it All Together

In each of these sections, we'll go over the final action points for how to implement this into your life. It is important to remember that you need to apply these to your individual life. Stoicism can seem specific but remember that it is not a religion. It is simply a philosophy that you can use to best help you find a virtuous path towards the good life.

The Distinction Between the Two Types of Virtue

In order to practically look at the distinction between the two types of virtue, make sure that you are constantly challenging your thoughts. You never want to get to a place where you just let your thoughts and your initial emotions take over.

When you are thinking something judgmental, such as "I hate my life," "her outfit is ugly," "that person sounds dumb," or anything else that can sound harsh like this, make sure that you stop and ask where that thought came from.

More often than not, you'll realize you don't fully believe in it at all and it's just a product of a value that you were conditioned into believing.

Eliminating Absolute Self-Talk

If something like "I never have any fun," "she's always on my nerves," or "everything is terrible," slips into your mind, remind yourself that one word can be too general for all the things that you actually know to be true.

You should correct yourself when you notice it's happening both in your thinking and your speech. Some will take a mental note when you correct yourself, so don't go out of your way to make sure you tell them how they should be talking. Others won't be so appreciative to get told how they should share their own information.

Do and Feel What is Appropriate in Every Circumstance

This step is all about "going with the flow." That can be an annoying phrase for those with anxiety, but certainly one that we have to remember. No matter how challenging it might be in any given situation, you have to make sure that you are being mindful. Naturally, you are going to think about the future, or maybe you will relate it to something that's happened in the past. As time goes on, put an emphasis on focusing on what's happening right now. Comparisons can help, but when you get too hung up on trying to figure out everything perfectly, that can be something that actually ends up setting you back.

Only Your Judgment Makes Something Either Good or Bad

The one true freedom that we have above all else is our ability to judge something. We get to decide whether something is good or bad.

Someone might punch you in the face, and there's no doubt that it will physically hurt.

They chose to do this to you, and you had no say in whether or not they were going to hit you, and whether or not it would physically hurt. Above all else, however, you will always hold the power to choose whether or not you get upset over it. You are the only one that holds the power to choose whether or not something is good or bad, in your eyes.

Nature has Always Been and Will Always Be Outside of Your Control

We have to start to learn how to let go of the things that we have no control over.

For a large portion of our lives, we spent a lot of time trying to change things, wishing for something better, and hoping that the future would be different.

What we didn't realize, however, is that we held the ability to effect change, but we were looking in the wrong places.

Make sure that you are always asking yourself whether or not you are living in accordance with nature.

Is that something that you can change, or is it another part of life that you simply have to learn to accept?

Do Not Be Consumed by Your Passions

Passion isn't something that we're just interested in. Passion can be an irrational reaction to the emotions that we are feeling. You can let passion drive you when you might react to a certain stimuli, but at the end of the day, it won't always be best to let your emotions do the decision-making.

Stoics are not empty of passion. Instead, they know how to control it. Rather than letting negative emotions control their passion, stoics are able to use their passion to emphasize the things that are good in life.

Always Avoid Being Excessive or Deficient

Many stoics will find that a minimalist lifestyle becomes more relevant to them. This doesn't mean giving away all of their stuff, rather, changing their perspective on how much stuff can actually make them happy.

Going forward, make sure that you are always checking in on whether or not you are being deficient, or excessive. When you feel like the amount that you are consuming something, or how much you are driving from a certain experience is not within the gray area, then you have to question if you are going over the limits. A stoic knows how to find the humble balance.

You Deserve and Require Evidence, Reason, or Proof

Never take anything for what it is on the surface. You do not have to obsess over the small details, and it won't always be your job to expose certain truths. However, it will be up to you, on an individual level, as you are defining your virtues, to require evidence, reason, and proof.

Even though you might feel as if it doesn't always matter, you are still deserving of this kind of knowledge. If we pretend that it isn't important, then we can lose sight of reality and start to only shape what we take in to please the comfortable perspective that we have created.

From the Overall Practice of These Eight Exercises

After you have begun to let these ideas in your life, you will start to realize that each thing becomes more defined. All your virtues are different, but as you shape your own perspective, you start to understand how they are really all connected in the end. Though one thing might seem more important at any given time, you will understand that all practices together make a harmonious, virtuous person.

What will Start to Happen as a result of Practicing this Strategy

Things in general will start to get easier. At first, you won't notice much of a difference. You will start to challenge your thoughts and combat your own way of thinking, and you might even feel more frustrated than you were in the beginning. The start of this is going to be a little more difficult.

Eventually, you will get to a point where it all just seems to click. The things that were more challenging in the past have fallen into place now, and you are no longer scared of what lies ahead. You will realize that when you go through painful experiences, it is never as terrifying as you made it out to be when you were still at a point when you were fearful.

Don't give up if you aren't completely happy at first, because that isn't going to happen. What will eventually occur is that you'll look back on yourself and become surprised at the way that you used to act. One day, you might run into someone in public that would have agitated you in the past, but you will become shocked that they don't even bother you.

People might even start to ask if something has changed. They will wonder if you are dating someone new, at a different job, or even taking medication. They might question why you are more relaxed, if something is wrong, or worry that you aren't as emotionless.

Eventually, they will realize that you are simply better at managing your feelings, and your stoic principles might even start to wear off on others.

What it's Like Before you Recognized This

Before you recognized these principles, you will have felt lost. You might still be feeling a little scared but remember that you have the power to change your way of thinking. Before reading this, you might have felt frustrated with the world, wondering if there was ever going to be something better.

How Things are Better Now as a Result of Practicing

Now, you understand that you have everything you need around you, it's simply the mentality that you are hoping to change. You will keep working towards something greater as well. Stoicism isn't about giving up on your dreams and just being comfortable. It's understanding that happiness is important in driving success, so learning to be satisfied with "the now," is what is actually going to help you find the better future.

An artist that criticizes every one of their paintings will never create something good. Someone overweight will never lose the pounds if they continue to belittle themselves and have low self-esteem.

A doctor that gives up on every patient will never help cure someone.

You have to learn how to be happy now, with whatever is around you, so that you can be even happier in a situation that is better. Stoics know that they need to feel emotion, and instead of hiding

that, they celebrate the fact that they can control the way that they are feeling.

Conclusion

By this point, you should have a solid understanding of what stoicism is. Remember, however, that it doesn't stop here. You shouldn't be satisfied with all the information you have now. You should be excited to do even more reading on the subject.

Start online if you have to. Places like Reddit offer great discussions. Even if they aren't from the most scholarly professionals, it's always nice to get your mind flowing when confronted with differing viewpoints.

Don't be afraid of the future anymore! You might also be overwhelmed at this point, worried about all the things you have to take in as they come. The more you start to learn, the more you realize just how much you have left to learn. This can be a challenging thing for stoics to confront, but as you continue to grow throughout this crazy world, you will start to appreciate all that you know.

Stoics can be satisfied with life because they are going to always be hungry for more philosophy. They will always question why they might have a thought, how something came to be, and what it can mean now. They won't agonize over these answers as other philosophers might and will instead be encouraged and excited about the endless opportunities that lie ahead.

The "Dos and Don'ts"

Do make sure that you never stop learning. Don't put limits on the things that you decide to take in.

Do forgive yourself for past mistakes. Don't ignore red flags or signs that negative behavior from the past is going to repeat itself now.

Do make sure that you are discussing your ideas with others. Don't condemn those for not believing in the same things as you.

Do share some advice when you think others are asking for it. Don't give unsolicited advice to individuals too consistently.

Do make sure that you are appreciative of all life has to offer. Don't be oblivious to the challenges and negative parts.

The Final Parting Tip

I encourage you now to take action. Do something that makes you question yourself. Look deep into who you are. I suggest by starting something new or going through a new experience. Take a small trip, or even go for a short walk somewhere you wouldn't have otherwise. Do something different to start to get your philosophical juices flowing, and if you can do it with nature, that's even better.

The main goal or theme of the entire book was to help get you started on a path towards the good life. What that looks like is going to be different in all people, but it is generally consisting of a world where we are always doing our best and showing passion, constantly seeking new information, and learning to accept life for what it is, with all its unexpected moments.

I want to wrap up with a motivational message seen through a final story that I think is powerful. Before I discovered stoicism, I thought of suicide often. I would think to myself, "what is the point?" It wasn't that I was actively self-harming, but I would often imagine suicide and all of the things that came along with those patterns of thinking. When I started to discover the philosophies of stoicism, it became much easier to break free from these ideations.

After a few years of stoicism, the thoughts of suicide stopped. It's not that I don't still understand what it means to have those feelings, or that I have lost perspective on the subject. Instead, I am focused now on growing and making sure that I am making the most of my future. I am too busy learning and growing to think of what it would be like if I ended that all now.

I challenge you to put this to use. Make yourself too busy for the negative in your life because you are emphasizing the positive. Don't allow yourself to give any more of your passion to the challenges of life. Instead, face them head on and focus only on the good, and doing good.

Let us know in a review how this has changed your life. We love to hear the stories of others and hope that you are able to share your journey with loved ones as well!

A final powerful quote that I think is important comes from one of the most important leaders of this movement, Epictetus, "For every challenge, remember the resources you have within you to cope with it. Provoked by the sight of a handsome man or a beautiful woman, you will discover within you the contrary power of self-restraint.

Faced with pain, you will discover the power of endurance. If you are insulted, you will discover patience. In time, you will grow to be confident that there is not a single impression that you will not have the moral means to tolerate." (Epictetus, 125 AD)

Values and Virtues: Aristotelianism in Contemporary Ethics, edited by Timothy Chappell

Meditations, Marcus Aurelius Letters of a Stoic, Seneca Discourses, Epictetus

References

AURELIUS, M. (2019). MEDITATIONS. RACE POINT PUB.

"Zeno of Citium". Britannica Encyclopaedia. Chrysippus – Internet Encyclopedia of Philosophy

Cleanthes' Hymn to Zeus, translated by Ellery, M., 1976

Dirk Baltzly (Feb 7, 2008). "Stoicism". Stanford Encyclopedia of Philosophy.

Epictetus, & Lebell, S. The art of living.

Epictetus. (2000). Enchiridion, Or Manual. [Place of publication not identified]: Infomotions, Inc.

Graver, Margaret (2007), Stoicism and Emotions, University of Chicago Press

Pigliucci, M. (2019). How to Be a Stoic. Retrieved from https://opinionator.blogs.nytimes.com/2015/02/02/how-to-be-a-stoic/

Plato, Emlyn-Jones, C., & Preddy, W. Plato, Republic.

Reinalda, R. (2014). Why You Should Never Use Absolutes. Retrieved from https://www.huffpost.com/entry/never-use-absolutes_b_4646420

Seneca, L., & Gummere, R. Letters from a stoic.

Sharpe, Matthew. "Stoic Virtue Ethics." Handbook of Virtue Ethics, 2013, 28–41.

www.ingramcontent.com/pod-product-compliance
Lightning Source LLC
Chambersburg PA
CBHW070052120526
44588CB00033B/1410